DANNY GAL

THE BELONGING PARADOX

HOW TO SOLVE THE GLOBAL EMPATHY CRISIS

ADVANCE PRAISE

"In The Belonging Paradox, *Danny Gal offers powerful methods for bridging divides in our increasingly polarized world. Drawing on his extensive work with Israelis and Palestinians, he reveals that transformative connection is only possible when we develop the capacity to see the human behind the perceived enemy – a skill that feels more urgent than ever. Danny goes beyond theory, sharing compelling personal stories and practical wisdom that make this book an invaluable guide for leaders, negotiators and changemakers seeking to create meaningful connections across divides."*

– **PROFESSOR DANIEL L. SHAPIRO**
Author of *Negotiating the Nonnegotiable*
Founder and Director, Harvard International Negotiation Program

"In this important book, Danny Gal distills decades of work building empathy between Israelis and Palestinians, showing that building trust with the 'other' is not a task limited to saints but a practice that all of us can – and must – take up if our world is to survive."

– **DOUGLAS A. JOHNSON**
Lecturer in Public Policy at Harvard Kennedy School
Former Faculty Director of the Carr Center for Human Rights Policy

"The root of many of our challenges is the experience of disconnection, both internally and with others. Danny Gal is someone I have long admired, who has taken his own lived experience of the paradox of belonging and found a way to lessen this estrangement, to build bridges across divides. This is a deeply personal and powerful book showing how empathy, listening and a connected leadership can transform not just our personal relationships and our organizations, but also wider society as a whole. In the increasingly polarized world we live in, this book presents a thoughtful and practical way to navigate our way forward."

– STEVEN D'SOUZA

Senior Partner, Korn Ferry, Leadership and Professional Development

"Danny's work played a meaningful role in helping me and key people in our organization evolve, build stronger relationships and improve communication as our company scaled. His ability to listen deeply, offer sharp insights and foster trust made a real impact. A great professional with a knack for bringing out the best in people."

– DANIEL LEREYA

Chief Product and Technology Officer, Monday.com

Published by
LID Publishing
An imprint of LID Business Media Ltd.
LABS House, 15-19 Bloomsbury Way,
London, WC1A 2TH, UK

info@lidpublishing.com
www.lidpublishing.com

A member of:

ISBN: 978-1-917391-14-6
ISBN: 978-1-917391-15-3 (ebook)

Cover and page design: Caroline Li

DANNY GAL

THE BELONGING PARADOX

HOW TO SOLVE THE GLOBAL EMPATHY CRISIS

MADRID | MEXICO CITY | LONDON
BUENOS AIRES | BOGOTA | SHANGHAI

CONTENTS

PROLOGUE

That evening, as I stood on stage at the plaza, the sight of thousands of people seated around one thousand round tables filled me with a surge of awe and determination. They had come from diverse backgrounds, identities and experiences to participate in the largest facilitated street dialogue the world had ever seen. Holding the microphone, I felt the power of leadership awaken within me like never before. Yet, I knew they hadn't gathered to hear me speak. They came to listen to each other, to reclaim a lost sense of solidarity and to co-create solutions for a better future. My role wasn't to give a speech, but to hold the space, set the right energy and create the conditions for true connection to unfold.

This moment, at the height of the social justice protest movement in the summer of 2011, marked a peak in my career. It was the convergence of my two primary passions, both professional and personal: connecting people beyond differences and social innovation.

As an organizational development consultant, I have spent the past 30 years delivering hundreds of hours of consulting, partnering with dozens of CEOs, senior executives and leadership teams at companies such as HP, Teva Pharmaceuticals, Monday.com, Intel and many others. Throughout my career, one central theme has guided my work: helping leaders and teams unlock their fullest potential by strengthening the connections between them. Whether navigating organizational change, fostering collaboration, or bridging divides, my focus has always been on cultivating deeper, more authentic relationships that enable people to thrive together.

As a social innovation entrepreneur, my work has been dedicated to closing social gaps and building bridges between groups in conflict. Leveraging insights from my consulting career, I have ventured into some of the most challenging environments, such as the Israeli-Palestinian conflict, where I facilitated transitions from fear and hatred to hope and co-creation. I headed the Israeli office of the NGO 'Center for Emerging Futures,' where, alongside a Palestinian partner, I co-facilitated dozens of 'Global Village Square' meetings – gatherings that allowed adversaries to meet as humans and form friendships beyond fear and stereotypes. I also led the NGO Kav-Mashve, which focused on integrating Arab citizens of Israel into the workforce, aiming to eliminate discrimination and inequality. Additionally, I supported numerous social entrepreneurs by establishing an incubator for social innovation ventures called The-Hub Tel Aviv (TLV).

Whether in my role as an organizational consultant or as a social entrepreneur, my focus has always been on lowering defenses, fostering genuine listening and restoring the creative partnerships necessary for both business success and positive social impact.

After completing my master's degree in social and industrial psychology, I had the opportunity to study public administration at Harvard Kennedy School. I was also part of the teaching team of Professor Otto Scharmer, the creator of the Theory U model, at MIT Sloan School of Management. These experiences provided me with a global perspective, revealing that despite our differences as individuals, nations and cultures, we face common challenges in what divides us and causes disconnection.

In *The Belonging Paradox* I share insights from both careers, bridging business and social impact to address pressing issues in organizations, societies and the global community. The world around us is burning – not everyone experiences this firsthand, but global warming, pandemics, terrorism, wars, refugee crises and social inequality will inevitably reach our doorsteps if we don't act.

This is why I felt the urgency to share the lessons I've learned in my career, hoping to inspire the leader within you to contribute to a better world by connecting people to themselves, to each other and to nature, beyond barriers like fear, stereotypes and competition

In *The Belonging Paradox*, I explore two central themes. First, our world is experiencing unprecedented levels of disconnectedness and polarization, leading to a global empathy crisis that demands urgent action. Second, solving the greatest challenges of our time requires us to foster a sense of belonging by bringing together diverse groups and working in genuine partnership. Yet, creating this kind of unity is one of the toughest challenges we face in our divided world. This book offers new perspectives on togetherness, belonging and the delicate balance between individuality and connection, while providing practical insights for building more empathetic and connected organizations, communities and societies.

A few years ago, I recall a visit to London where I met close friend of mine from a Sikh origin. I recall asking him with curiosity why Sikhs wear turbans. His response struck me: "We had a king who declared that everyone should wear a turban because you are all kings." This message resonated deeply with my belief that leadership is for everyone, not just a select few. We all have the potential to step up, take responsibility and make a difference, regardless of gender, race or background.

Join me on this journey to rediscover the leader within each of us through personal experiences and thought-provoking insights. I will share stories both from my personal and professional lives that will shed light on how to find balance between our need for self-expression and our need to belong – the essence of *The Belonging Paradox*. This is an urgent call to address the empathy crisis that is threatening our organizations, societies and our world, and to take meaningful steps toward a more connected and compassionate future.

HOW TO READ THIS BOOK

This book explores the Belonging Paradox – the ongoing tension between our need for connection and our desire for individuality. Throughout, you'll see words like balancing, navigating and mastering, but these don't imply a simple solution. Paradoxes are complex, dynamic forces that challenge us to hold two opposing truths. This book is an invitation to actively engage with this tension, using insights and practical examples to shape the world around us without expecting a clear-cut solution.

As you read, bring a sense of curiosity. Each chapter offers perspectives and stories that you can adapt to your own life. You may find yourself pausing to reflect, question or challenge ideas along the way – this is part of the journey. Together, let's explore how embracing this paradox might open new possibilities for connection and belonging in a complex world.

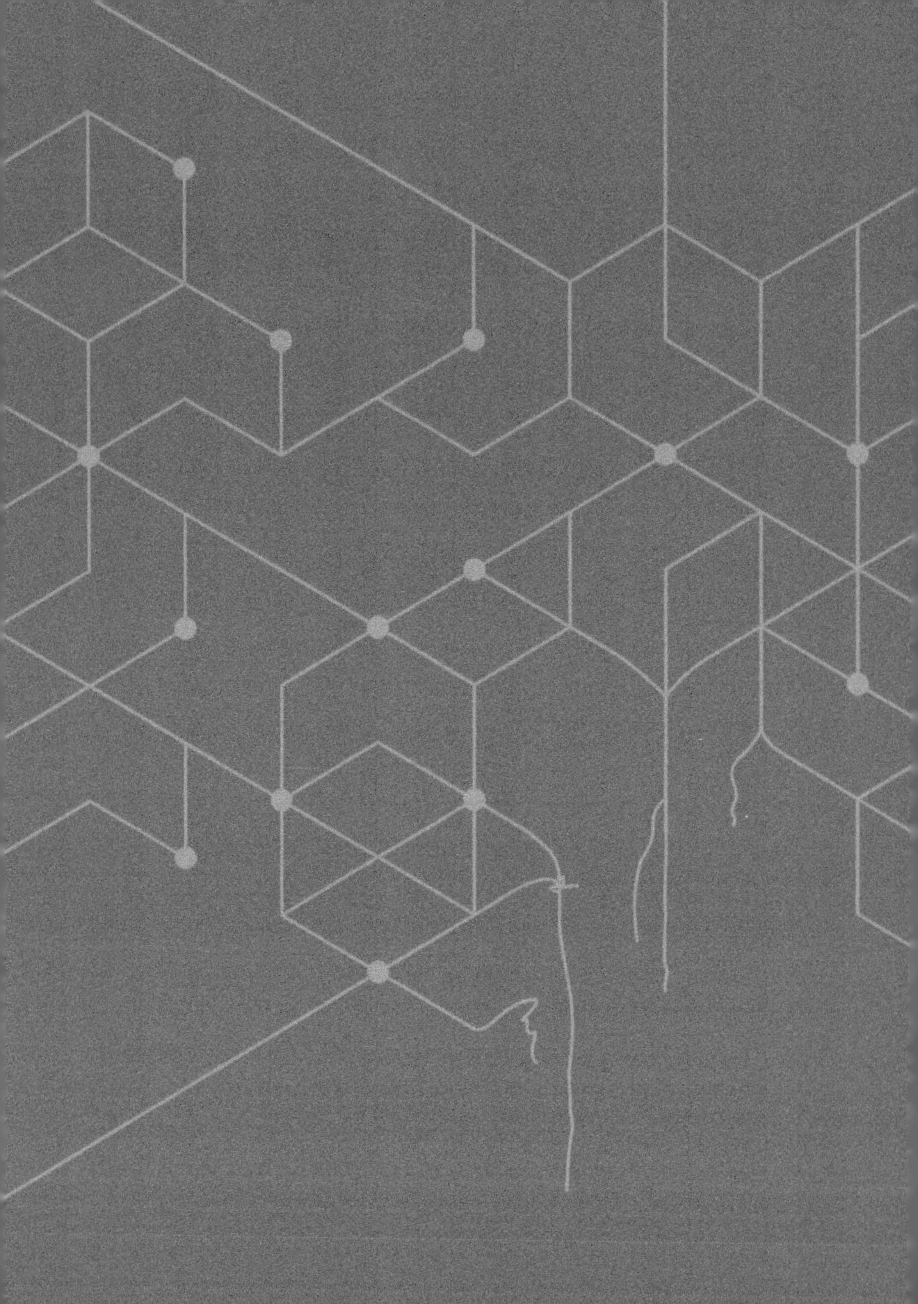

CHAPTER 1

INTRODUCTION

To be like everyone else and also to be unique: these conflicting forces to both assimilate and stand out have operated within me since childhood. They are impulses that exist in each of us, reflective of our human nature. I call this ongoing tension 'The Belonging Paradox' – the challenge of balancing our need for uniqueness with our equally strong desire to belong.

Everyone is born with a unique fingerprint. They possess external and internal qualities that make them unique and special. At the same time, humans are social animals, with a biological and evolutionary tendency to belong to groups. We live with perpetual tension, striving to establish our uniqueness at the same time as trying to fit in. In this book, we will explore how balance can be achieved and the importance of such balance at every level of humanity, from the personal to the global.

A CHILD'S PERSPECTIVE

The home in which I grew up was the home of Holocaust survivors, where parents did not talk about what happened during the war because they wanted to protect their children, avoiding the horror stories of the recent past. But everything was bubbling beneath the surface. As a child, I sensed the things that were not talked about and internalized the need to be sensitive, careful and always on guard. The Nazis could come at any moment and the end of the world was a distinct possibility.

My mother was a baby in 1939. My grandmother had to carry her in her arms as they fled Warsaw, only days before the Nazi invasion. As a young child, mom was so hungry that she learned to grab every piece of food thrown on the ground before the rats did. Her father had died as a soldier in the Russian army, so she didn't have a chance to know him.

My father was only three when his family was forced to move into the Warsaw Ghetto. There he witnessed the Ghetto's Jewish population shrink from 300,000 to less than 20,000. At the age of seven, during the Warsaw Ghetto Uprising of 1943, my father had to crawl through the sewers and navigate in the dark to escape the Ghetto. He won his freedom but could never leave behind what he had witnessed.

I was born in Israel two years after the Six-Day War of June 1967, then, at the age of four, lived through the Yom Kippur War of October 1973. During my childhood, the Holocaust and its legacy hung in the background while to the fore was the story of the State of Israel, its survival and revival. Conflict and its disastrous consequences never seemed far away. I remember how in the evenings we had to shut off the apartment's lights and darken the building to avoid becoming a target for the enemy's bombers. I also remember how, each evening, we had to leave our sixth-floor apartment and sleep with neighbors on the lower floors, closer to the bomb shelters. My father returned safely from the war but there were friends whose fathers never returned.

As a child, I tried to understand why the Nazis had wanted to extinguish people like me. Numerous other questions swirled in my head: Why were we so often at war with the neighboring Arab states? Why was our relationship with the world so difficult and complicated? Why, closer to home, did my parents frequently fight and yell at each other? Why didn't people get along with each other? How was it possible that people who didn't seem to like each other were still able to build huge bridges and skyscrapers, to fly to the moon and engineer incredible vehicles like Ferraris and Lamborghinis? I was as curious as any other child confronted with the complexities and contradictions of the world, sharing what I discovered with others.

TRYING TO FIT IN

My parents spoke Polish at home, which meant I grew up fluent in that language, which was quite unusual among Israelis for whom Hebrew was the first language. I had blond hair and my aunts and grandmother would affectionately refer to me as a non-Jewish "Goy." While this infuriated me, they intended it as a compliment: looking as I did, the Nazis would never take any notice of me. It was unsettling to be told this. When I started school, I made every effort to hide my Polish roots, trying to look like a regular kid. But it took time and effort to learn how to hide my Polish accent, especially the way I rolled my Rs. My distinctiveness remained, though, despite my best efforts to fit in. I could not hide who I really was. Over the years, I learned to accept this distinctiveness as a unique gift rather than as an obstacle to belonging.

In 1977, when I was in third grade, there was an event that everyone who lived through that period will never forget. President Anwar el-Sadat of Egypt, considered by many a great enemy of our nation, visited Israel. This unprecedented visit by an Arab leader opened a peace process between Israel and Egypt. Writing this, my eyes tear up as I recall sitting with my family before the black-and-white TV set watching the President emerge from his plane and being welcomed by the Israeli Prime Minister Menachem Begin and former Prime Minister Golda Meir. It was an unbelievable moment that demonstrated that even the worst enemies can find ways to reconciliation.

Egyptian President Anwar Sadat and Prime Minister Menachem Begin in serious talks at the King David Hotel diner in Jerusalem, 1977. Photo by Government Press Office (Israel), via Wikimedia Commons, licensed under CC BY-SA 3.0.

The next day at school, the teacher asked us to draw a back perspective of a child waving the Israeli flag and a dove. Hundreds of children's drawings were placed on a wall in our local town museum, forming a "Peace Collage" that celebrated Sadat's visit. All the children drew a child from the back as they were told. Only I drew a child in profile. For years when I passed by the collage, I saw my distinct drawing as if it was me hanging there on the wall showing my otherness. That's how I was. Different, sometimes unusual, sometimes hiding myself, ashamed of my strangeness, sometimes proud of it and happy that it led to unexpected and interesting connections. I didn't always belong but very much wanted to. Like the child in my drawing, I watched on from the side, viewing the world from the sidelines.

ALIENATION

On many occasions, both as a child and an adult, I found myself feeling alienated because of my uniqueness, even though I desperately wanted to belong. At times, I thought it was just me. But as I grew older and listened to others' stories, I realized that many people had experienced the same struggle: feeling misunderstood, different and struggling with low self-esteem, while outwardly pretending to fit in and not show how lonely and vulnerable they felt. As adults, the challenge may be less openly dramatic than in childhood, but the tension between belonging and experiencing the world differently remains a central part of who we are. This tension lies at the heart of the Belonging Paradox.

Alienation and loneliness are experienced by more people today than in the past. A report on the loneliness epidemic (Cinga 2021) found that 58% of US adults are considered lonely, with an increasing number of people feeling left out, poorly understood and lacking companionship. People are eager to belong but are finding it increasingly difficult to accomplish. Technology supposedly connects us. In practice, however, it often creates more distance and alienation. We no longer need to leave home to manage everyday necessities. So much is now at our fingertips, accessible 24/7 via a computer or smartphone. If we do leave the house, we find that the urban environments that we traverse are designed and engineered in a way that captures our attention, bombarding us with endless distractions. Consequently, we engage with fewer people and find temporary satisfaction through such activities as web-browsing, shopping and eating.

For many, home feels safer, more familiar and less challenging. But along with this comfort comes loneliness, lack of belonging and detachment from society and environment. Today, it is more difficult than ever to be part of meaningful groups without risking your sense of safety and personal boundaries. Many people choose to keep their own company. Others choose to practice belonging by being part of larger symbolic groups, such as political parties and religious communities. These provide meaning and comfort, but sometimes this is at the expense of self-development and personal uniqueness.

Alienation and personal detachment are symptoms that affect people on a personal level. However, the accumulative effect threatens the resilience of our societies and is evident when groups of people, societies and nations don't find constructive ways to live together.

A DISCONNECTED WORLD

Global challenges present an existential threat not only to humankind but also to the entire planet. Many of these crises stem from the conflict between individual ego and the collective good. This often manifests in humanity's struggle to extend generosity beyond personal or cultural boundaries, as well as the failure to honor and respect the natural environment. These deep-rooted tensions highlight the difficulty of embracing a shared responsibility for the future, one that transcends tribal divisions and environmental exploitation.

On a local and personal scale, that might not seem very threatening, but when it occurs across a community, a city, a nation, or at a planetary level, its effects are more noticeable and harmful. The complex, frequently interacting, challenges are manifested in the environmental disasters, military conflicts and steady flow of refugees who flee economic deprivation and seek new homes in other nations; in the ecological catastrophes and climate crises signaled by deforestation, desertification, ocean acidification, plastic pollution and irreversible temperature rises; in the social polarization and antipathy between ethnic and partisan groups that often results in civil unrest and violent suppression in many countries; and in the economic divide that sees the very rich, who represent 1% of the global population, holding the same wealth as the poorest 50%. These are all issues that arise from the imbalance between the interests of the individual or specific-group and the benefit of the whole. The inability to recognize the bigger picture and act with a broader awareness leads to global challenges that must be addressed collectively.

The global crises we face today can be seen as manifestations of 'The Belonging Paradox' on a massive scale – where the pursuit of individual or group interests often clashes with the collective good. From environmental exploitation to social polarization, the inability to find a balance between personal freedom and shared responsibility threatens our shared future. The challenge lies in navigating this paradox to foster both a sense of community and respect for individual expression. If we fail to do so, these unresolved issues will become the unfortunate legacy we leave for future generations.

These symptoms cannot be ignored even if not all of them affect us directly now. If we wait, it will be too late. Advances in transport and communication have made the world a smaller place. What seems distant today can show up on our own doorstep tomorrow. We see this with the impact of terrorist attacks, with the effects of economic disasters, with the behavior of viruses, with the gradual rise in sea levels. The 9/11 attacks in the United States, the fallout from the Great Recession, the global spread of the COVID-19 pandemic and the erosion of coastlines and terminal flood threats to islands and cities all illustrate our interconnection and shared vulnerability. They highlight the need for global community and action. These are complex problems that we cannot solve alone but may be able to tackle together.

Collaboration is one of the most complicated and challenging processes. While our default position tends to be competitive, with occasional cooperative endeavors that deliver mutual benefit, failure to collaborate is fatal. Collaboration relies on shared goals and purpose. Implicitly, collaborative action must be beneficial to and respectful of all the parties involved. This applies both to the dynamics within those parties and to the relationships between them. Nations must constantly work on finding new ways for national cohesion as a response to the polarization and mistrust between diverse groups. Countries must find ways to overcome ego and past trauma to collaborate over burning regional issues. People must learn new ways to be together, otherwise we will simply be replaced by other species that can co-habit more effectively than we can.

THE ROOT OF THE PROBLEM

The urgency to write this book was born out of the concern that human togetherness is failing. It often leads to disastrous consequences for which we need to take responsibility. Nevertheless, there are beliefs, knowledge, practices and tools that can enable the togetherness the world needs. We need to "crack the code" of togetherness, facilitating common action for the benefit of us all. No matter the scale – family, community, city, society, nation, planet – we must join forces and act now.

To achieve this, we must start by going to the root of the matter, exploring what we mean by *togetherness*, the conditions under which it flourishes and the benefits it delivers to people, nature and planet. In doing so, we must understand the Belonging Paradox – the tension between our polarized needs to belong and to express our unique selves – and recognize the creative and destructive potential within this paradox. Too much emphasis on distinctive uniqueness and it is more difficult to build coherent togetherness, while too much emphasis on togetherness makes less space for anyone to express their personal uniqueness. Neither extreme serves us well, so finding a healthy and fulfilling balance is what we must aspire to.

Consider a couple's relationship. The more someone is assimilated into a dyadic relationship, talking and thinking as a couple, the more they neglect their personal development. On the other hand, the more they invest in personal development, growing in unique and disconnected directions, the more they may distance themselves from their partner. Sometimes this can lead to separation. This tension – between maintaining a meaningful connection and nurturing individual identity – demonstrates the Belonging Paradox. Relationships highlight the delicate balance needed to cultivate togetherness without sacrificing uniqueness, but rising divorce statistics illustrate how challenging this balance can be.

Sports teams are another example of the required balance between individual talent and collective effort.

Players work hard for their teammates, often placing teamwork above self-expression, as selfishness can hinder team goals. However, true success occurs when personal talents are allowed to shine within the framework of teamwork, as seen with superstars like Lionel Messi and Michael Jordan. A winning team finds the right balance – too much consideration of others harms competitive drive, while excessive individualism weakens group achievement. Finding and maintaining the right balance is key. This is the magic sauce of any team, not just in sports. But this balance is constantly tested by human egos and shifting group dynamics.

NAVIGATING THE BELONGING PARADOX

Researchers in social psychology have observed the tension between an individual's actions to advance their goals, agency, and their actions to promote group belonging, communion (Bakan 1966). In other fields of psychology, different naming conventions have been adopted (Entringer 2022): dominance vs nurturance in personality psychology; competence vs warmth in social psychology; independence vs interdependence in the psychology of the self; and attachment vs authenticity in the field of trauma and addiction, as explored by Gabor Maté.

Individuals, communities, organizations and societies that manage this paradox in an effective and conscious way benefit and experience both the pleasures of connection and belonging as well as the ability to express and practice their individual unique identity.

When someone finds their balance in this paradox, they feel like they fit in. They experience a sense of belonging, of finding a home, of being seen and accepted for who they are, without biases and without pressure to change. It is a situation that leads to creative flow, an optimistic feeling that all the pieces of the puzzle magically have fallen into place. The opposite state makes us feel that we do not fit, that something in us or in the situation is incomplete and lacking in harmony. Lengthy exposure to this state can lead to a decrease in personal effectiveness, depression, seclusion and apathy.

Finding the balance within the paradox is more a feeling than cognitive process. It can be felt, for example, in a concert hall when, for a moment, the entire audience experiences a shared excitement, as if goose-bumped skin and hearts were interconnected, linking conductor, orchestra and audience. Teams with the most talented players, whose results are poor, tend to lack the balance that accompanies this state. Here the strength of ego undermines connection and coordination, and the possibility of magic is lost.

The Belonging Paradox applies to every level of human society, from the personal and local to the national and global. Democracy, for example, is the most common method of social organization in the West. Nevertheless, while it is the most successful method in nations where individual freedom is a fundamental value, it does not lack problems in how it operates. The idea that the majority rules can sometimes pose a threat to minority groups and deny them their rights. In addition, when complex issues are voted on, opinion and voting preferences can be manipulated through fake news, social media influence and targeted advertising. Democratic societies can make bad decisions that do not benefit their future.

If we view democracy through the Belonging Paradox lens, a healthy democracy is one in which every citizen has the right to self-determination, personal expression and creative freedom. Citizens are expected to show consideration for others, practicing responsibility for the common good. Yet the COVID-19 pandemic reminded us that finding the right balance between self and society is not an easy task. Confronted by the crisis, we expected our governments to act in ways that would create wide protection against the virus through vaccines, closures and mandating collective action such as mask-wearing and social distancing. However, there were people who refused to take the vaccine or wear masks, insisting on their fundamental rights and freedoms, many of them enshrined in law. Where can the balance be struck to contain the pandemic while honoring freedom of choice? Where is the balance between mutual care and self-interest? Between belonging and individuality? And between compromises for the common good and pursuit of personal goals and desires?

These are questions that will inform the content of this book. Life is complex and there are no easy answers or magic solutions. Each of us must learn to navigate, the Belonging Paradox constantly balancing our need for personal expression with our desire to belong. The initial chapters that follow will deal with understanding the psychological mechanisms that underly the Belonging Paradox, examining the implications and applications for individuals, couples and families. In subsequent chapters, we will explore how the Belonging Paradox scales to the level of teams, organizations and human society in general. We will discover that achieving balance between belonging and uniqueness can only ever be contextual and temporary. We must constantly adapt and change. At the age of fifty-five, I am still learning this, gaining more insights about myself and my place in the world. Indeed, this is a journey that does not have a fixed destination but one in which pleasure is derived from what is learned along the way.

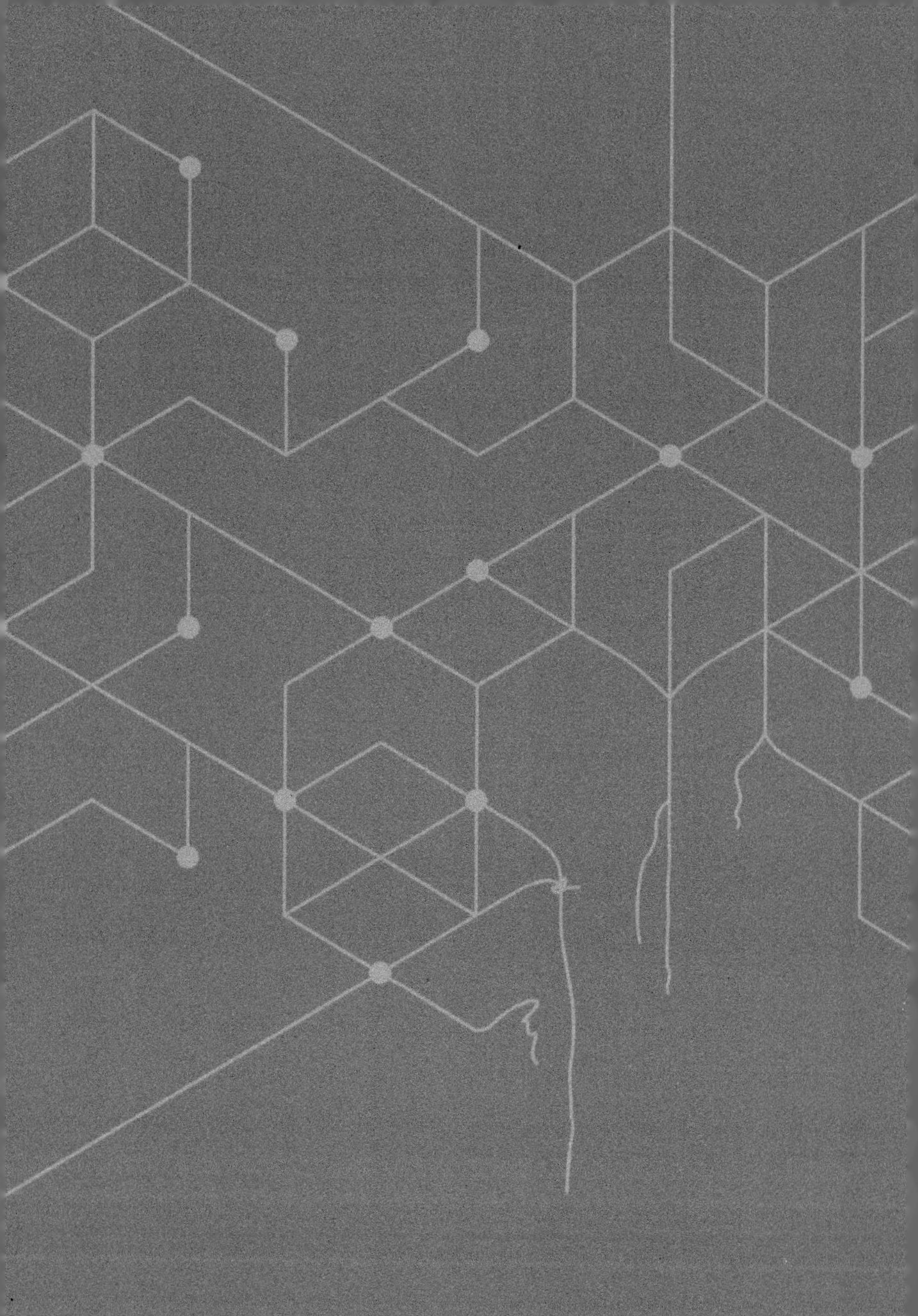

CHAPTER 2

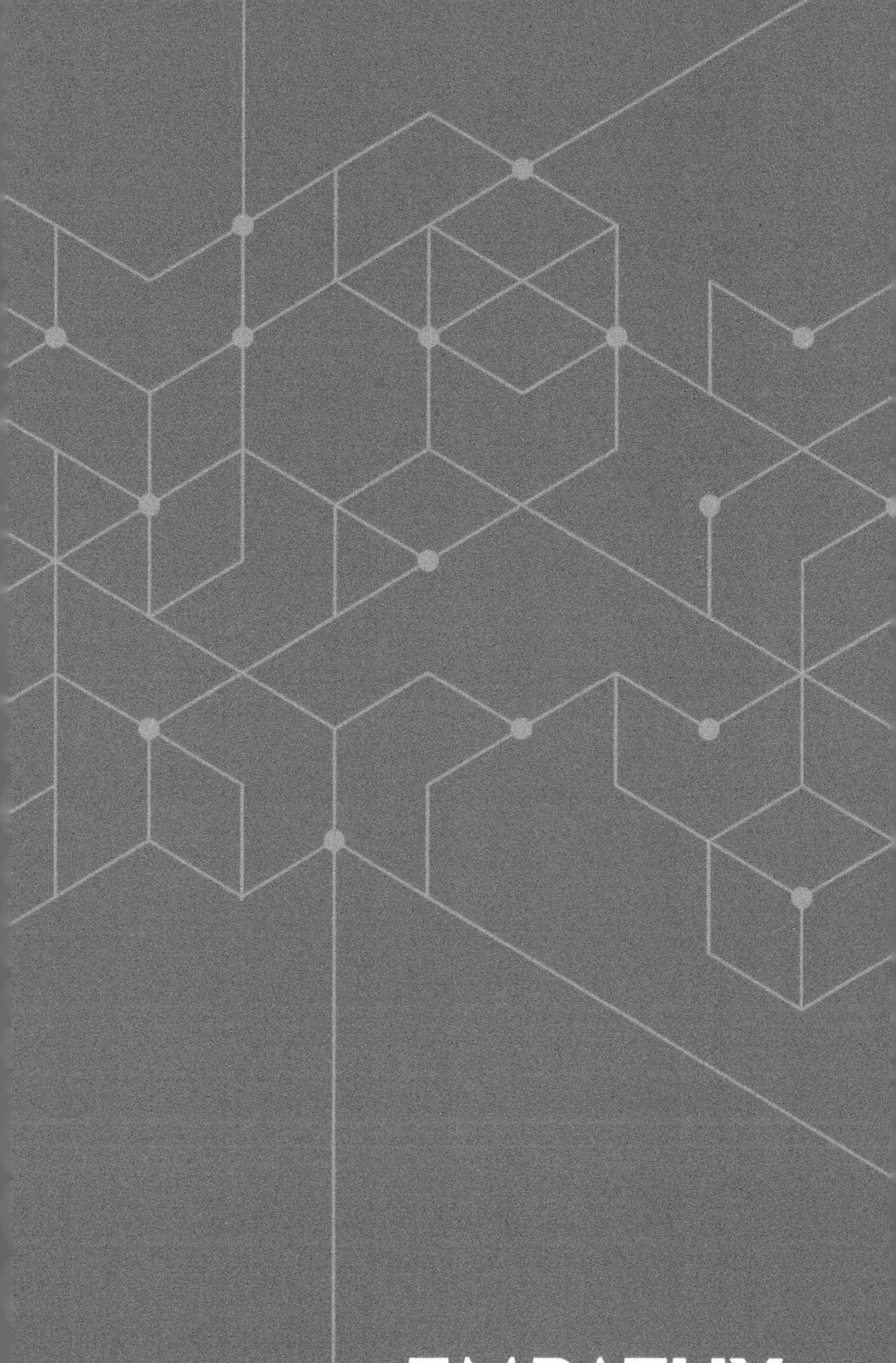

EMPATHY

When I was aged four or five, I remember watching other children in kindergarten and thinking, "He is not me." I can still recall the feeling when I recognized that the other was different and separate from me, as well as my curiosity about what was going through their mind. As I grew up, I retained this curiosity, becoming sensitive and attentive to other people and their emotions. I would notice nuances in tone of voice, facial gestures and energy, sensing that my own feelings tended to mirror what others felt.

In my teens, I earned my status among my peers, both male and female, as a listener. Sometimes, I wanted to rid myself of this role and just be light-hearted and flowing. With time, however, I understood it to be a strength that gave me confidence. Listening became central to my life, my career and my relationships with other people.

THE PHYSIOLOGICAL FOUNDATION FOR EMPATHY

All human beings are physiologically wired to feel the other. Among the brain's important components that enable this are mirror neurons. Newborns, for example, respond to the crying of other babies around them. Our brains respond electrically and chemically to the signals of others, long before emotions and cognition have an effect. When we see other people distressed or joyful, we may also experience these feelings because of mirror neurons.

EMPATHY DEFINED

The ability to experience the other emotionally and mentally, to see the world as they do, is known as empathy. The Merriam-Webster dictionary defines *empathy* as "the action of understanding, being aware of, being sensitive to and vicariously experiencing the feelings, thoughts and experiences of another of either the past or present without having the feelings, thoughts and experience fully communicated in an objectively explicit manner."

This definition implies that empathy has several components: emotional, cognitive and behavioral. The emotional component is related to the ability to feel, share and respond to the other's feelings. The cognitive component is related to the ability to understand the other's emotional state and to attribute the right name to this feeling. The behavioral component refers to a person's action in response to understanding another's condition and context.

EMPATHIC DIFFERENCES

Different people are born with different levels of sensitivity toward the other. Some people are hypersensitive to others and can be identified as over-empathetic. Such people respond immediately to any facial expression, tone of voice, or even an invisible change of energy. There are two facets to this hypersensitivity. On the one hand, it allows people to be very precise in how they read the social environment, in how they develop understanding of complex situations and in how they adapt. On the other, it burdens them, making interactions with others unbearable and creating a pressing need to disconnect.

Conversely, there are people whose levels of sensitivity to others are severely impaired. Generally, they are thought to be indifferent or insensitive. In more extreme cases, such people lack social skills and are unable to interpret social situations. These characteristics are sometimes found in people on the autistic spectrum. A recent study (Chan 2020) suggests that mirror neurons in individuals with autism operate differently compared to those without autism, pointing to potential differences in how actions and emotions are understood and mirrored in social situations. On the other hand, individuals referred to as sociopaths may experience a limited or inconsistent capacity for empathy, often showing little concern for the wellbeing of others, but they may still understand social cues and emotions when it suits their own needs.

HOW EMPATHY DEVELOPS

Parents who are attuned to their babies' needs and show them warmth and love inspire confidence and trust in those children. They grow up capable of sensing the needs of others. This is where the emotional layer that sits on top of the physiological (neurons) layer develops. As a baby becomes a child, the cognitive (understanding) layer develops. Thoughts such as "he is not me" are suggestive of how children notice themselves as separate entities with their own thoughts and feelings. During the next stage, the behavioral layer develops. Withing this layer lies the ability to translate sensations, feelings, emotions and thoughts into actions.

The first significant relationship a child experiences is with a parent or carer. We are born completely dependent on caregivers and have no ability to survive without them. When a baby is in distress, an adult provides the solution. This is how a baby learns that there is someone who responds to their call and helps them to relax. In psychological terms, the confidence and trust fostered by these actions is known as *attachment*. This is the beginning of a long and complex relationship between the child and the significant adults in their life. The more accurate the parents' response to the baby's needs, the more secure the attachment develops in the baby. By accurate I mean that if the child's diaper is wet, feeding is not the best response, and if the child just needs some love or tenderness then a pacifier is just a partial remedy.

Attachment provides the basis for a child to develop relationships with and empathy for others later in life. The caregiver instills a model of love and care in the child's operating system. In optimal situations, the child will develop emotional regulation mechanisms that, as an adult, will enable them to regulate emotions and see the other, especially in stressful situations. Empathy allows children to notice and respond to unpleasant situations that involve their friends, relatives, or others in their immediate environment. It is not unusual to see children aged two or three caressing or hugging another child who is crying.

While this suggests imitation of parental behavior rather than premature evidence of empathy, the *identification* of distress in another child is the critical point here.

BETWEEN EMPATHY AND SYMPATHY

Empathy enables us to establish and manage healthy relationships. Our ability to sense and to listen helps us to understand what prompts specific behaviors in other people. Empathy is neither mercy nor sympathy. The ability to feel the other does not require full identification with that person. I can have empathy for someone without necessarily agreeing with them. When we feel sympathy and identify with the other, we coalesce with that person and cannot maintain the separation that is so important to the relationship. Without a certain level of separation, of selfhood, it is hard for individuals to maintain their emotional independence and they become enmeshed with each other. The result is like a boundaryless soup of emotions. Empathy is the ability to feel the emotional state of the other without losing your independent self and without being overwhelmed.

Balancing the Belonging Paradox is not possible without empathy. Empathy is what helps us be part of a group and community. Without empathy we will have a hard time accepting those who are different from us, especially when difference leads to friction and conflict. Empathy is crucial to balancing the paradox because it comes from a place of separation and not from a place of over-identification. When the latter occurs, it becomes a restrictive experience, fomenting a blurred sense of belonging that does not allow enough self-expression, causing the individual to be absorbed by the whole. This kind of absorption is often found in cults and dictatorships. It contrasts starkly with the democratic model founded on equality and individual self-expression.

A world without empathy is extremely dangerous and is no less critical to the individual than global warming or famine. Empathic failure is at the base of most current global challenges as articulated in the UN Sustainable Development Goals (SDGs).

Empathy is the foundation of how we connect, yet in today's world, it is under serious threat. Our increasing reliance on technology and the pressures of modern life are eroding this essential human capacity. In the next chapter, we will explore these challenges and understand why empathy is becoming an endangered quality – and why it is vital to protect and nurture it for our shared future.

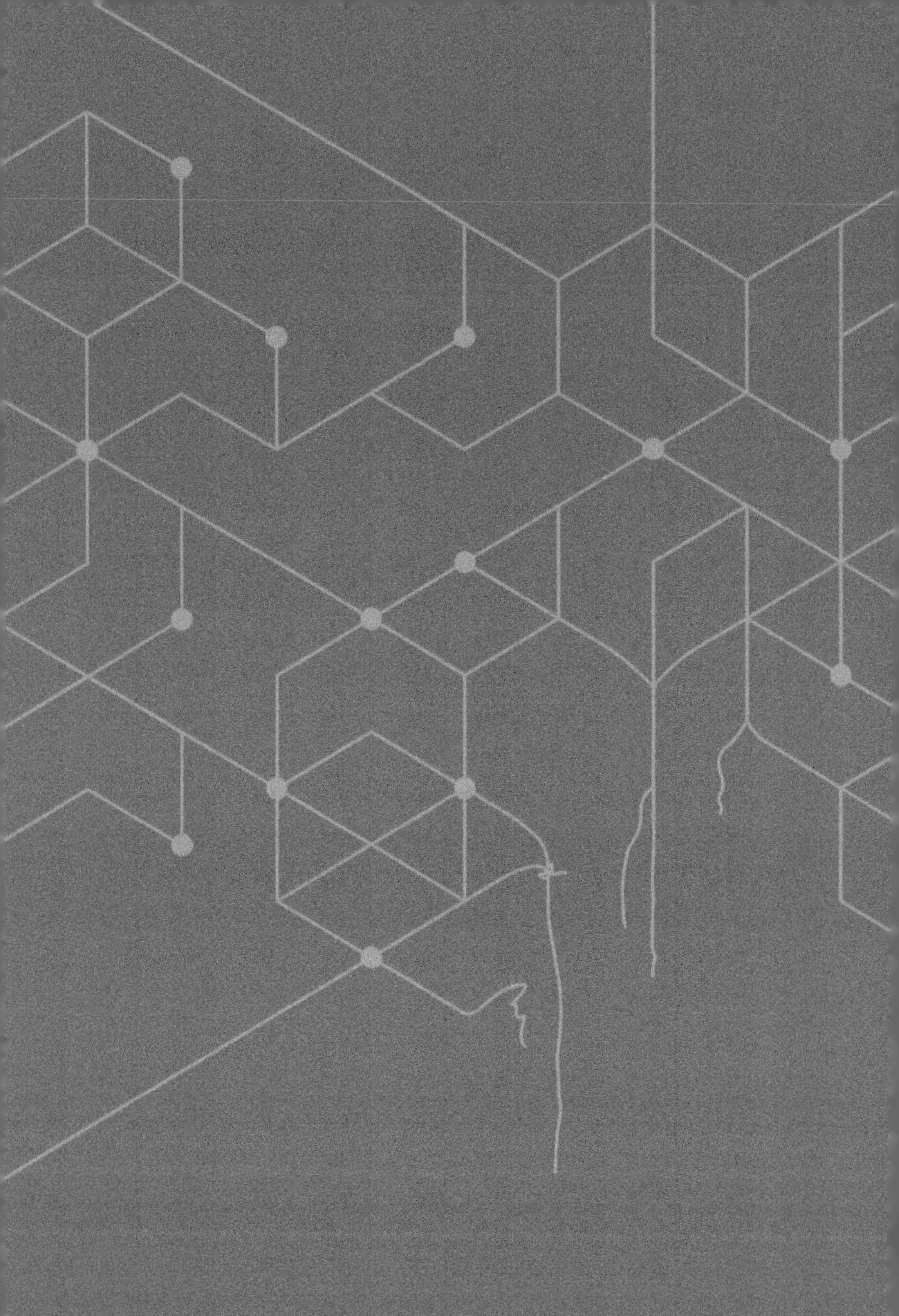

CHAPTER 3

EMPATHY: AN ENDANGERED HUMAN CAPACITY

ADDICTION TO TECHNOLOGY

Many books and articles I read begin with sentences like: "We live in times of information flooding ... we are constantly bombarded with millions of stimuli, and our minds are not built to deal with it ..." I feel that way too. As our attention is grabbed by screen-based technologies, we lose our serenity. This is evidenced by people's widespread addiction to smartphones and social media, and by children who prefer playing virtual games to spending time outdoors.

At the start of the COVID-19 pandemic, I naively wondered whether this was nature's way of giving us a break, inviting us to re-examine our habits and intensity of life. It was not long, though, before there was an intensification of digital and virtual activity. Instead of breaks, we spent whole days in front of screens, changing meetings but not location. I am sure that I am not the only one who suffered with headaches because of screen radiation, information overload and poor diet. The pandemic exacerbated the situation rather than alleviating it.

COLLECTIVE ATTENTION DEFICIT DISORDER

Since the late 20th century and increasingly so in the 21st, we have all been affected to varying degrees by the phenomenon known as attention deficit disorder (ADD) or attention deficit hyperactivity disorder (ADHD). Although recognized in the *Diagnostic and Statistical Manual of*

Mental Disorders (DSM-5), the official classification publication of the American Psychiatric Association, there are many researchers who suggest that such disorders are rooted in sociology rather than biology. For example Sami Timimi, who is an NHS child and adolescent psychiatrist, argues that ADHD is not an objective "disorder" but is a consequence of societal pressures and environmental causes (Timimi 2009). This begins with young children who are presented with too many choices for toys, screens and clothes. Such abundance of stimuli is not always positive, as constant distractions impair the ability to focus and derive enjoyment from deep immersion in a single object or activity. As children grow older and start to access their own digital devices, they are exposed to the risk of uncontrollable addiction to the online world, which can make everything offline appear dull. Adults, too, even as they restrict their children's screen time, find themselves caught up in an endless loop of social media posts, text messages and smartphone app content.

SCREEN INFLUENCE

The giant companies responsible for many of these apps and online services made their fortunes with advertising-oriented business models. This despite being better known for the provision of other services, such as search engines and social media platforms. To sell advertisements, organizations like Facebook (Meta) and Google must constantly refine their technology to ensure maximum advertising exposure, whether conscious or unconscious. To this end, they have engineered processes that demand screen-based attention and the consumption of content that enables their advertisement sales.

There are some similarities with the approach to TV advertising, although there is a significant difference in terms of both addiction and level of awareness. TV viewers often use commercial breaks as an opportunity to disconnect and walk away, making a drink, having a snack, or visiting the bathroom. With the internet, though, the challenge is different, with commercials catching our attention more accurately and powerfully than those on TV. This is because Google, Facebook and other companies have detected patterns in the way we use the internet and what interests us, what we like and what we are likely to buy. They now profile and target us with personalized advertisements that influence and tempt. This is a process of automatic and continuous refinement as corporate internet-based systems learn more about us, our preferences and behaviors.

The distraction of internet-based advertising has become increasingly sophisticated over the years. Often, we no longer consciously notice the influence of online adverts or, where we are conscious, we find them useful, legitimizing them even as they manipulate our actions, online purchases and brand awareness.

If distractions and consciousness engineering were only in the realm of advertising, we might have found ways to deal with them as we did with TV commercials. However, the giant companies are not satisfied with merely using targeted advertisements. They want to ensure we stay glued to our screens to consume them and, to achieve this, they have devised more creative ways to keep us engaged. One example of such a trick is when you press the "back" button on an Android device while browsing your Facebook feed. In most applications, the back button takes you out of the app and returns you to the home page. In Facebook, however, it takes you to the top of the feed and presents you with a new stream of posts and attention-grabbers. You usually do not notice this manipulation because they do an excellent job of placing content at the top of the feed that aligns perfectly with your interests. On iOS, the back button trick doesn't exist, but they use other methods to keep users engaged, such as push notifications, infinite scroll, stories and reels. Consequently, in a subliminal way, most users fall victim to these "glueing" tricks that keep them perpetually engaged.

Another dangerous way to grab our attention is to focus on improving the non-commercial content that appears in our feeds. With personalized user profiles, the tech companies can filter non-commercial content that will attract our attention. This is done in a way that will not upset us, that remains aligned with the way we think and that is intended to strengthen predetermined beliefs. For example, people whose profiles indicate that they identify with left-wing politics will see more content and posts from organizations and people who share their political views. The same thing happens for those on the right side of the political spectrum. User satisfaction leads to command of user attention, which then generates advertising revenue.

These methods also have led to interference in elections and the distortion of public opinion, prompting suspicions, for example, about the role played by online services in the lead-up to the US elections of 2016 and 2020 and the Brexit vote in the UK. Their use is growing exponentially and, at the time of this writing, no one appears to be stopping or regulating such practices. Over the years, the internet giants have undertaken a nonpolitical but extremely influential invasion of personal privacy and private attention. This invasion, which is occurring 'under the radar,' poses one of the most dangerous threats to humanity.

ANESTHESIA OF EMOTION

The pace, relevance and accuracy of the posts that we are exposed to greatly increase our addiction, weakening our awareness and ability to resist. Beyond that, the urge to constantly move on to the next thing, to a new stimulus, causes us not to stay with what each post evokes in us, preventing our emotional systems from doing their work. Someone can sit in front of a computer and read posts about wars, natural disasters, animal abuse, rape and so on, surfing from post to post without stopping to reflect, notice and feel at any level that goes beyond the superficial. The steady flow of new information, spiced with commercial baits, dulls emotions and blurs feelings in a gradual process of zombification. The less we are aware of and sensitive to our own feelings, the less likely we are to be able to feel the other. As a society, we become desensitized and lacking in empathy.

THE SOCIAL FABRIC IS IN DANGER OF DISINTEGRATING

We've gone far beyond the boundaries of advertising. Tech giants are shaping our consciousness and controlling the way we see the world. If we rely too much on their engineered sources of information, our understanding of reality becomes biased and less empathic toward those who don't resemble us or share our views. Over time, we become more closed-minded and less curious. When we have less information and familiarity with what and how others think, we are more affected by manipulative information designed to intimidate and constrain us. Through lack of understanding, we tend to demonize and fear the other. The danger is that without a basic level of empathy, we will lose our ability to live together and share our planet. This is equally as dangerous as other global threats such as climate change, pandemics and wars.

COLLECTIVE EMPATHY DISORDER

The empathy disorder develops as we spend more time in engineered virtual spaces. Barack Obama, the former President of the United States, often speaks of "empathy deficit," observing that it is more serious than economic deficit. As this deficit affects all human beings, there is a danger that the ability to feel empathy will decrease drastically. Although the capacity for empathy lies in our genes and brain structure, if we do not practice and develop it, it will remain dormant and useless. Sadly, social network addiction continues to erode this capacity. Today, many people cannot navigate without the assistance of digital apps such as Google Maps and Waze. Humans have become increasingly dependent on such tools, inhibiting the development of their innate navigational capability. The same thing is happening with empathy.

THE KEY TO A HUMAN SOCIETY

Empathy is critical to society, community, family and any other social structure. In his book *Sapiens*, Yuval Noah Harari explains why humans, who were negligible and insignificant animals 70,000 years ago, were able to reach the current state in which they are the strongest species on Earth. Harari's theory emphasizes the ability of human beings to cooperate with each other in diverse and flexible ways. Unlike other creatures, such as wolves, starlings and bees that can do things together in a synchronized way, humans know how to imagine, using abstract ideas and stories that are not necessarily grounded in reality, to create an emotional and cognitive connection. Humans know how to listen to each other, read signs and find solutions together. Listening and empathy have allowed humans to connect creatively and find solutions to nature's challenges in ways that no other animal has been able to.

EMPATHY VERSUS IDEOLOGY

Imagination is what allowed humans to build larger societal structures and grow beyond the village community. Humans can invent stories and convince each other. Certain stories and shared imaginaries are particularly compelling, such as a belief in the existence God or a belief that money in the form of a metal coin or piece of paper has value in exchange for goods. Social myths and collective imaginaries allowed humanity to organize into large groups of "believers," developing rules of conduct, values and laws. These systems enabled the creation of huge societal structures like religions, cities, nations and corporations. These structures, organized around a common story or a belief, hold more power than any individual or unorganized group.

It is worth reflecting on the difference between organizations that are based on personal acquaintance and empathy and other organizations that are based on shared stories and beliefs. The former allow for intimacy, compassion and a sense of community. These tend to be small-interest groups, teams, tribes, communities and villages. Larger organizations cohere around a common story (a national ethos, for example), belief (the story of Jesus), or vision (the corporate aspirations of Apple or Disney). These allow for economic and political power and are typical of ideological movements, religions, countries and corporations.

When ideology is a stronger source of connection than empathy, it can lead to destructive and disastrous results. Exploited by totalitarian regimes, ideological emphasis can very quickly give way to fear, as evidenced by countless historical examples, such as Nazi Germany. Human organizations that are founded on empathy prioritize relationships between people. The basic building block is the small community that connects with a wider system of communities, contextualizing the local in relation to the global.

Empathy is embedded in our DNA. Nevertheless, there is a huge empathic gap between people who are not able to see the other's suffering and acknowledge it. Without this it is difficult to find common and satisfying solutions. While our stories and the actions they inspire can be good for some people, they can be catastrophic for others. In the wake of the Holocaust, for example, the establishment of Israel as an independent state was a cause of celebration for the Jewish people, but also the story of *Nakba* (disaster) for the Palestinian people.

The decline of empathy is an alarming trend in today's world. As our attention is increasingly consumed by technology and engineered stimuli, we become less capable of genuinely connecting with others and more susceptible to division and misunderstanding. Reversing this trend requires a conscious effort to nurture empathy – starting with how we engage in our daily interactions.

At the heart of fostering empathy lies the art of listening. Listening deeply, both to ourselves and to others, is what allows empathy to flourish and communities to thrive. In the next chapter, we'll explore how listening is not just a skill, but a transformative process that shapes our relationships and helps us connect on a meaningful level.

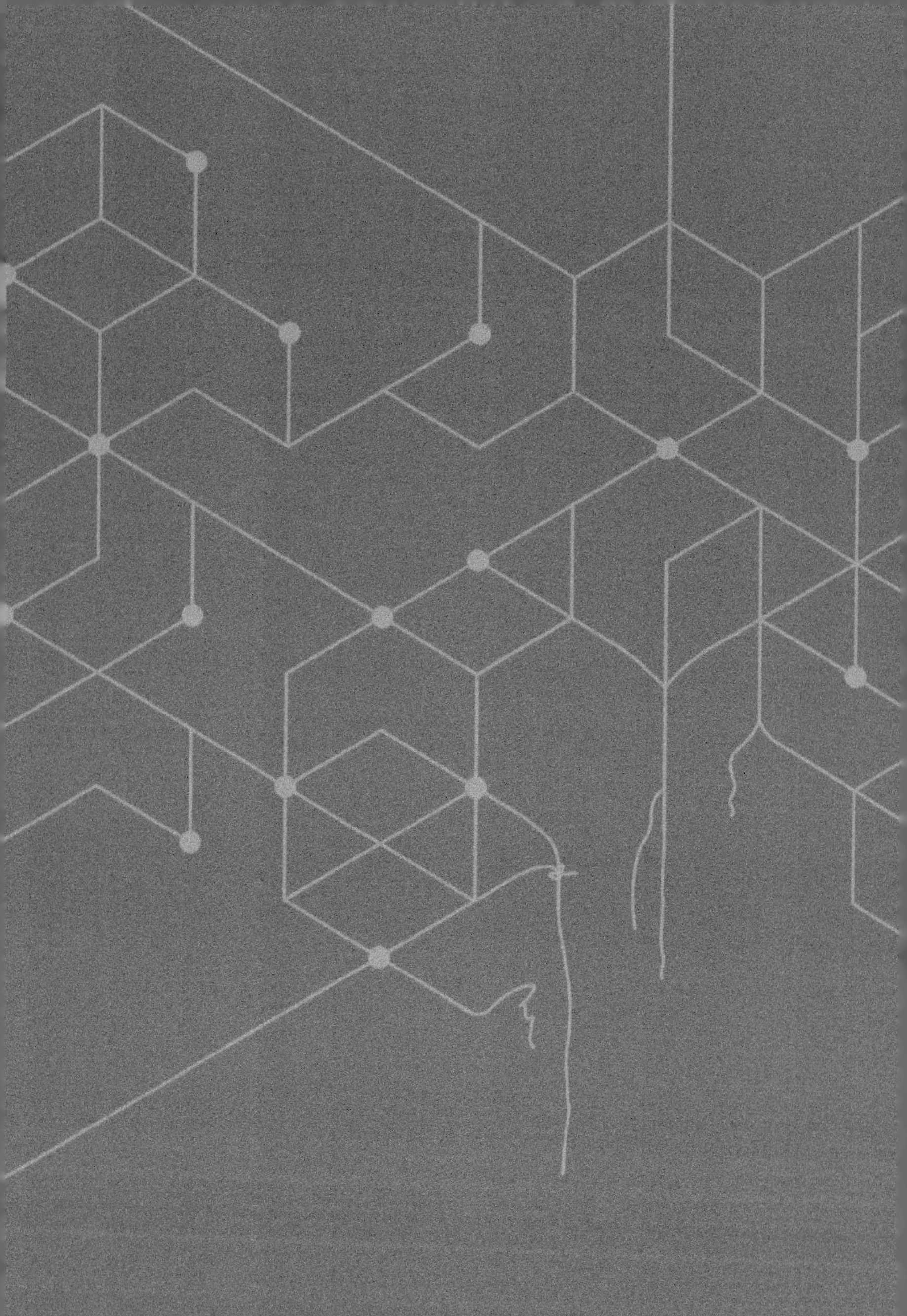

CHAPTER 4

LISTENING

THE BEGINNING OF MY PROFESSIONAL PATH AS A LISTENER

As a teenager, I enjoyed listening to others. I noticed that my listening helped friends open up and feel good about themselves. Ours was a special high school that encouraged its graduates to enroll in the military academic reserve and pursue technological excellence. Many of my classmates followed this path and went on to become leaders in the high-tech industry in Israel and abroad. However, I was more passionate about psychology than technology or mathematics. This led me to study the topic at the Tel Aviv University and then join the military as a behavioral science officer. At first, I served as a research officer, but I was soon invited to become a military organizational consultant, which has subsequently evolved into a lifelong career.

As I immersed myself in the organizational consulting profession, I quickly realized that listening was the most important skill that I would utilize. As I grew older and gained experience, I learned to listen more deeply and noticed how, in addition to encouraging openness, this enabled people to grow. This was an intuitive ability, stemming from personal sensitivity and supplemented by the theories and research I absorbed about listening. I felt that the more I understood the listening mechanism, the better I could both listen to others and teach the craft of listening, extending the reach of this essential practice.

LISTENING AND ATTENTION

"You do not listen" is something that people who are in a close relationship - whether between friends, spouses, parents and children, or teachers and students - often say to one another. We are all familiar with the situation where we hear what is being said but it does not really penetrate our outer shell, making others feel that we are not listening. Listening is more than just physical hearing. It requires that we pay close attention and devote energy to what we hear, as well as to what we see and sense. When we do this well, listening creates a pleasant sense of caring, even if we do not fully understand the message or disagree with it.

During the early years of my relationship with my spouse, Rachel, she taught me a lesson about listening. At times, she would share a concern or a dilemma with me and my instinct was to listen and understand, then to offer my opinion or suggest a solution. I did this because I cared and believed it would be understood as a gesture of love. To my surprise, Rachel didn't feel comfortable with this type of listening, which also involved analysis. She asked me to simply listen and be with her while she told her story. This kind of listening is often more difficult as it counters our personal need to be seen as wise or helpful. It also highlights the challenges of focused attention in the face of other distractions. In Hebrew, *listening* (בישקהל) is derived from the root בשק, which is the same root as *attention*. To pay attention is a core ability that enables listening. This kind of presence is something that can be developed and trained. First, though, we must learn that listening to others starts with listening to ourselves.

LISTENING TO OURSELVES

Listening recognizes the other, allowing them to feel heard and seen. To listen to ourselves, we must be aware of an inner voice that wants to be heard, reconnecting with what our body, our inner wisdom, is trying to tell us. This is difficult because often what the inner voice tells us is uncomfortable. To avoid being disturbed, we allow ourselves to be easily distracted by the world around us. The more the inner voice is silenced, the more we permit ourselves to become addicted to habits that distance us from our true selves. Yet the inner voice is critical to our ability to be authentic and healthy. How, then, can we break this cycle and reconnect to our inner selves?

Occasionally, caught up in the relentless bustle of life, we all experience those momentary pauses when we suddenly notice the smell and color of flowers, the sound and movement of birds, the lyrics of a song playing on the radio. We notice, too, how these things move us, making us feel excited. These rare and important experiences take us off 'autopilot,' however temporarily, and enable an emotional connection both with the world around us and with our inner selves. When we experience such moments, it is important to notice and stay with what triggers us emotionally and intuitively. Our body knows, beyond the cognitive layers, what we are longing for. Paying attention to this is a form of mindfulness.

There are plenty of resources on mindfulness which can explain the practice and importance of being present and listening to ourselves. These explanations are beyond the scope of this book. In essence, though, it is about awareness of our inner voice, making us more focused and attentive. Listening to ourselves enables us to become attuned to the environment and to other people. When we are present, we listen from a place of connection and coherence. In this way, listening to ourselves becomes the foundation for listening to others. When we understand these two forms of listening as part of one listening system, we begin to appreciate the art of listening in a deeper way.

FOUR LEVELS OF LISTENING

According to Otto Scharmer, MIT professor and author of *Theory U* (Scharmer 2009), there are four levels of listening. Navigating between these levels is an art. Those who have mastered it can both listen to others and remain connected to the deepest potential of self, other and the wider world. This is important because unique belonging requires that we master all types of listening to allow our uniqueness to integrate into the whole in a manner that is mutually beneficial.

1. **Level 1 – Downloading**: We hear and validate what we already know. At this level of listening, we are not really open to the new or to anything beyond our original perceptions. It is like downloading the files that are already stored in our system.

2. **Level 2 – Factual**: We listen to new information, taking note of what is different from what we already know. To be able to do this we must pause our instinctive judgment that is often activated when we encounter facts that shake our own structure of knowing. This is what Scharmer calls 'open mind.'

3. **Level 3 – Empathic**: We can see the situation through the eyes of the other, with high awareness of their emotional state. To listen empathically, we must enter our 'open heart' zone and feel the other.

4. **Level 4 – Generative**: This is a bi-focal form of listening, bringing together empathic listening with our own inner place. The magic happens when the two focal points create a trembling effect that suggests that there is a potential concentration of energy here. Noticing this and staying with this feeling for a while can lead to strong insights and self-revelation. We listen during this 'open Will' phase to an emerging possible future that wants to be born.

THE IMPORTANCE OF THE FOUR LISTENING LEVELS

During the Downloading phase, you mostly listen to yourself, responding to what you hear from the outside. Your attention is primarily on yourself. During the Factual phase, you listen to the external flow of information through an intellectual prism and notice what's new. At both levels, you concentrate on yourself and what you already do and don't know. Listening is through the head and self-centric. During the Empathic phase, you shift the focus of attention from yourself to the other. You do not necessarily have to agree but you are able to understand and feel the other's perspective. This is the typical situation for caregivers and sensitive people who excel at listening to others. This form of listening is not always connected to yourself and your deepest needs. During the Generative phase, you manage to hold two centers of attention simultaneously - the internal and the external (empathic) - as well as the space of potential between them. This is the potential for something significant, something that lies half-awake at the dawn of consciousness.

RESONANCE

In generative listening, the frequency of the object you are listening to 'outside' meets your internal frequency, and the encounter between the frequencies creates what in the science of physics is called resonance. We are familiar with the phenomenon of resonance from everyday life. When we push a child on a swing, we adjust our push frequency to the frequency of the swing and then the altitude is increased with every push. If we lose our rhythm, balance is lost, and the movement of the swing slows. In another example, it is possible to shatter a glass with sound alone. Experienced singers can adjust the frequency of their voices to make this happen.

In English, it is customary to say, "It resonates with me" when we listen to something that makes an inner string tremble within us. The generative phase of listening invokes such trembling, taking us out of our comfort zone and shaking our inner status quo, challenging our identities and the stories we tell ourselves about our lives.

WHAT WANTS TO DIE AND WHAT WANTS TO BE BORN

Generative listening can signal that something wants to be born within us. The disruption is so significant because usually this new life can only emerge if we are willing to let go of something else that was well rooted in us. Generative listening, therefore, involves paying attention to what is ready to die and what wants to be born, "learning from the emerging future," as Scharmer phrases it. In this moment lies the seed of a potential future, as well as fear and the possibility of missing the moment. Fear is a coping mechanism that tries to maintain the status quo and is change-averse. Curiosity in the face of fear, however, can provide a glimpse of the emerging future and of the change that can affect all our lives. Generative listening is important during special moments in our lives, when big decisions need to be made and when it is time for change.

In the language of the Belonging Paradox, generative listening is the tool that helps us know where and when to belong, as well as when it is time to move on. Empathic listening is what helps us cope with diversity, especially in the groups that we belong to. Without it, disagreements create tension and conflict that make belonging impossible. Factual listening is important for noticing the different perspectives and sources of knowledge that exist and being able to pick them up for the sake of both group and self. Downloading listening happens when there is too much routine and lack of change or when the situation is unstable, and people are looking for reassurance. There is nothing wrong with this kind of listening if people can become more attentive and less self-centric when required. These four levels of listening are foundational to Balancing the Belonging Paradox. A healthy form of belonging requires that people achieve a balance between contributing to and receiving from other members of the group.

LISTENING TO THE INNER SOURCE

Scharmer's *Theory U* is a positive leadership model that focuses on creating a better world (or 'Tikkun Olam' in the Jewish tradition). It advocates a leadership style that is in service of the common good, reduces social conflicts, promotes a healthy environment and increases people's connection to themselves and their loved ones. Scharmer's study is based on in-depth interviews conducted with one hundred prominent business leaders. It reveals how, beyond rational-analytic thinking, many leaders rely on conscious connection to an inner source of wisdom. This shapes the decisions they make and the action they take. Two people, Scharmer's research suggests, can do the same thing in the same way, yet achieve completely different results. The only difference will be an internal state of consciousness, invisible from the outside.

When I first encountered Scharmer's insights, they did not resonate with me. That changed over time as I began to reflect on the moments when I made my most important life decisions. In some cases, I could recall the feeling of a deeper knowledge, of a deeper connection to myself, as if I was a channel for an ancient source of wisdom. In other cases, I made decisions based on fear, social comparison, or ego. It became clear to me that when I was connected to my inner wisdom and had a sense of clarity around my deeper mission, I made better decisions for myself and for everyone around me.

However, when I was stuck in entrenched patterns, not listening to what was happening inside me, my actions often achieved the opposite of what I intended. When I was a director at a nongovernmental organization, for example, I facilitated monthly enrichment and learning meetings. One involved a simulation exercise that aimed to develop awareness of and improve our teamwork. But people emerged from the exercise tenser and angrier than they had been, responding to what they perceived as my hidden agenda. Unconsciously, I had acted from a critical inner place, and this had riled my colleagues.

On another occasion, during a trip to Catalonia to celebrate my son's Bar-Mitzvah and watch Messi play against Ronaldo in El Clásico between F.C. Barcelona and Real Madrid, I frequently pointed out sunglasses stores to him enquiring whether he would like a pair. Finally, my son's patience snapped, and he pointed out that it was me rather than him that wanted new glasses. As with the reactions of my work colleagues, his observation made me more aware of my inner source of action.

Mastering the art of listening, both to ourselves and others, is essential for deep connection and meaningful relationships. Listening helps us understand the unique qualities that make each person who they are, fostering empathy and building healthy bonds. But how do we take this understanding of ourselves and use it to make our individual presence stronger, especially within a group or community?

In the next chapter, we will explore what it means to fully embrace our uniqueness in a way that enables us to belong authentically. We will see how our individual stories, backgrounds and personality traits can become platforms for connection and growth – both for ourselves and for the communities we are part of. This is the essence of *mastering the Belonging Paradox* at the individual level.

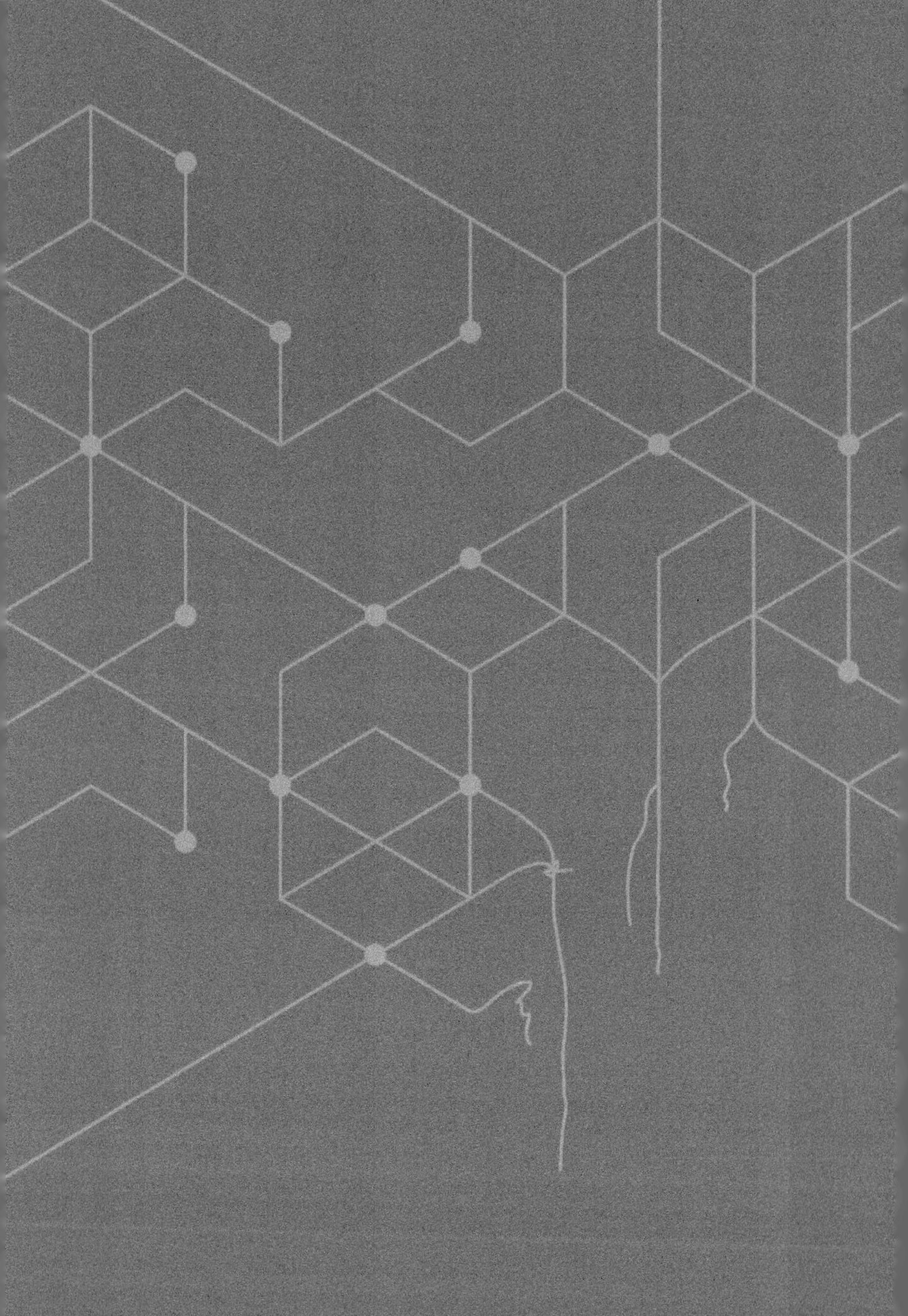

CHAPTER 5

THE BELONGING PARADOX AT THE INDIVIDUAL LEVEL

When I worked at Kav-Mashve, the NGO aimed at integrating Arab degree holders into Israeli businesses, meeting and learning about the lives of the students we served was one of the highlights of my job.

Abeer, a courageous young woman from a small Arab village in the north of Israel, is one individual I remember well. Growing up, Abeer had always dreamed of becoming a businesswoman who worked in Tel Aviv or another overseas business hub. But in her village, she had no role models for this type of lifestyle, and her family pushed her to become a teacher and stay nearby. Even when she was admitted to the prestigious Tel Aviv University, her parents didn't really think she'd ever move out of her village. While Abeer was determined and ambitious, her first year at the school was a nightmare. She was always the best student in class, but she felt less capable than her colleagues and was often very lonely. She faced a host of challenges, including a language barrier, minority status, the necessity of navigating cultural subtleties, and the enormous differences between the ways the university and her local high school functioned. These were significant enough that she thought about dropping out. Luckily, Abeer joined a special student group called the Arab Business Club (ABC), organized by Kav-Mashve. In it, she met other students in similar situations and, together, they formed a support group that helped them survive that first year.

When I met Abeer, I was impressed by her high standards and ambition. But I knew she was struggling. She told me that she and her Arab colleagues always sat in the last rows of the lecture halls. She said they seldom dared to ask questions during lectures for fear of looking silly and that they were generally too embarrassed to approach the lecturer after the class. Feeling isolated by their differences, Abeer and her Arab friends created a sort of 'bubble' for themselves, which meant they engaged even less with other Israeli students from the majority (Jewish) group.

Abeer's story is typical of the students I met and worked with. The experience of feeling different and strange as part of a minority group leads to isolation, seclusion and not realizing one's full intellectual and social potential. Nearly 100% of the Arab students and graduates I spoke with, like Abeer, reported a major crisis during their first year of university studies – a crisis that made them consider dropping out or changing professions. Those who persevered developed personal resilience and the ability to overcome difficulties independently. While this resilience aided their further studies, it also reinforced the trend of seclusion and separation.

Instead of the educational experience serving as an opportunity for students to connect, create a social network and lay the groundwork for future job prospects, the opposite occurred: students were forced to confront challenges alone, and they failed to build confidence and faith in themselves and their abilities to overcome social and intercultural barriers. Consequently, after graduation, while students from the Jewish majority group moved on to seek and secure employment, most Arab graduates were unable to find jobs in their fields of study. Abeer, who had done well in her legal studies, started to feel the pressure from her family to return to her village and follow the traditional career path laid out for her rather than try to find a job in the leading law offices of Tel Aviv.

Abeer's story and the stories of her colleagues are examples of an unfortunate trend. Despite the growing number of Arab students in Israeli higher education, we have not seen a corresponding increase in their integration into the Israeli labor market.

This phenomenon is not unique to Israel. Belonging to a minority group can sometimes inhibit the fulfilment of a person's potential within the larger context of any community or society. Why is this? And what can we do about it? This chapter will examine how our individual stories, backgrounds and personality traits can be used as a platform for connection and success rather than for isolation.

SEEING THE POTENTIAL IN YOU

During my meetings with students, I asked them to tell me their life stories. I had them talk about their backgrounds, the influence of their local environments and the significant events that shaped their present-day identities as adults. After listening to each story, I would offer a reflective summary of what I heard and what I perceived to be the narrative's impact on who they were. The students' responses to my reflections were surprising. One young man said, "Wow, this is the first time someone has really listened to my life story and helped me understand it."

The others agreed. They were not used to being seen as individuals with dreams, wishes and unique presences.

In those moments, I considered how challenging it would have been for me to grow up and reach adulthood without anyone acknowledging me as a unique individual and attending to me in a personal, empowering and non-judgmental manner. I began to wonder why this happened among some groups of people and not others.

I quickly learned that cultural factors play a role. In collectivist societies, such as the traditional Arab one that Abeer was raised in, there tends to be less focus on each person's individual identity and greater emphasis placed on the extended family. Each individual in the extended family assumes a role within the family hierarchy. This role (eldest sibling, future doctor, promising young person, supportive sibling, etc.) comes with certain expectations, and the individual is often perceived through the lens of these expectations.

Hassan, for example, had been expected to become a doctor since childhood. He was the promise of the family and the best and the most diligent student. Hassan's family never asked him if he wanted to be a doctor, and Hassan didn't ask himself this question either, even when he visited a sick relative at a hospital and felt dizzy from the smells and sights he encountered. After he was admitted to one of Israel's best medical schools and was preparing himself for the long academic road ahead, he started working in a restaurant to pay his tuition. One week before the start of the academic year, a restaurant coworker accidentally cut his finger. When Hassan saw the blood, he instantly felt sick and panicked. After taking a pause, he stepped outside of the restaurant to gather his wits and started to think about the significance of this event. He decided not to go back home that day. Instead, he asked his boss for his week's wages, went to the airport, and bought a one-way ticket to London. Basically, he ran away from his destiny. He stayed and worked in London for years, getting to know himself and what he really wanted without the pressure of family expectations. In the process, he became much more mature. After five years, he was ready to return home knowing exactly what he wanted: to be a computer engineer. While not many young people have the courage or the means to do what Hassan did, his situation – one of not knowing who he really was and what was his inner calling was – is very typical.

When I engaged with each student as a unique individual through these conversations, a transformation occurred. They began to see themselves in a new light. They started granting themselves internal legitimacy to be who they wanted to be. This marked the beginning of a lengthy process, assisted by the talented instructors at the association, which ultimately led to a crucial outcome: students started to dare to see themselves as 'worthy,' envisioning themselves in leading workplaces without feeling inferior to other candidates.

This realization indicated to me that the first crucial step toward helping 'different' individuals integrate is assisting them in believing in themselves and recognizing their value as individuals. Healthy belonging must start with a healthy self-perception.

STRANGE OR UNIQUE?

The challenge of seeing oneself as a unique and valuable individual is not exclusive to those who come from minority groups. Nearly everyone faces the realization of being different at some point in their lives. Effective coping can lead to a sense of uniqueness, which brings appreciation and recognition. Less effective coping, however, can result in viewing oneself as a 'strange exception.' This perception is often accompanied by low self-esteem. Since we are all different and unique, it is essential that we learn to cultivate a sense of uniqueness rather than abnormality.

I learned this firsthand when I reached the age of Bar Mitzvah in the Jewish tradition. All my friends began studying with a rabbi as part of the Torah acquisition process that typically culminates in a special ceremony at the synagogue. My secular parents discouraged this. I recall initially feeling embarrassed. I was jealous of my friends who were following the traditional path, and my parents knew it. One day, my mom said to me, "I see that you are sad about not preparing for a Bar Mitzvah. So, your dad and I thought that we should find another meaningful way to celebrate your 13th birthday together. We thought we'd do a coast-to-coast trip in the US instead. What do you think?" My eyes lit up. I had never been to the US before and eagerly chose to travel. The experience was very special, and it showed me that there were many ways to celebrate this life transition. After that, I started to be proud of my parents and of myself. I realized that being different could be unique. We had an original way of thinking that didn't just follow what everyone else was doing. Instead, we critically examined each tradition and custom, making choices that were aligned with our values and worldview. This has become a tool in my personality toolbox – an important tool for a child who started out shy and felt like he had to hide his Polish roots to not be rejected and ridiculed.

THE VOICES THAT KEEP US FROM CELEBRATING OUR UNIQUENESS

In these situations, what Abeer, Hassan and I had in common was the ability to flip the story we told ourselves and feel unique and worthy with our different paths. In looking back on my own development, I realized that, to make this shift, I needed to recognize and master the dialogue that so often happens in our heads. I saw that there were three inner voices deep within all of us that can get in the way of our ability to see the value of our contributions. These are: the voice of criticism, the voice of comparison and the voice of fear.

THE VOICE OF CRITICISM

The foundation of embracing our uniqueness lies in our ability to see ourselves with loving and noncritical eyes. This can be challenging, as the critical voices we encountered during our childhood linger within us and continue to activate us. While these voices cannot be eliminated entirely, we can seize moments when the critical voices speak up and turn them around to acknowledge and appreciate the treasure trove of qualities, abilities and mental strengths we possess.

Omer, one of my consulting clients, is a senior executive at a high-tech firm. He tends to be very critical toward his employees and always sees the glass as half-empty. When we discussed this behavior, we went back to his roots. Omer had a father that always criticized him as a way to challenge him. As a result, Omer felt like he was 'not enough' for his father. He developed an obsession with proving his father wrong and, at the same time, he also internalized an inner voice that constantly told him that he was not enough. This voice continued to live in him and was reflected in his lack of satisfaction with his employees. To change this pattern, Omer took responsibility for practicing self-appreciation and forgiveness. He understood that he could not change his external behavior without winning over the voice of criticism inside him. I coached Omer to have a dialogue with this inner voice. He would speak to it internally, saying: "I know you, and you always tell me that I'm not good enough, but you are not a part of me. You are an external voice that has infiltrated my system and remained there. I release you." This conscious recognition and dismissal of the critical voice helped alleviate its impact, allowing Omer to focus on his unique strengths and qualities. Today, Omer is leading his team in a much more appreciative manner without lowering his standards of excellence.

While we might not all have critical voices as vocal as Omer's, we all have some version of this voice. It's important for us to learn to recognize how and when this voice appears in our lives. Then, we must learn to acknowledge it and manage its impact to ensure that we are able to see the beautiful and successful sides of our individuality. In other words, the ability to look at yourself in the mirror and love what you see is crucial for the ability to see the good in others.

THE COMPARATIVE VOICE

Comparative voices constantly hold us up to others and conclude that others are better, more attractive or more successful.

Like critical voices, comparative voices are habits that can be changed. While they cannot be eliminated entirely, we can become aware of them and their impact on us. These voices tend to hinder us, causing us to stop dreaming, desiring and attempting new things because we assume we will fall short.

For example, my daughter really wanted to learn to play the guitar. But every time she tried to practice, she believed that her playing was so 'bad' compared to her friends (who had started long before her) that she would give up. I couldn't persuade her that she needed to be patient and that progress would come over time, and she stopped playing altogether for a year.

Then, one day, I took her to a concert of the Israeli singer-songwriter Efrat Gosh. My daughter adores Efrat Gosh and, while she was at the show, she turned to me and said: "Dad, I want to be like her, and I understand it takes a lot of time and work to get there." As a result of this experience, her attitude and approach totally changed. She started to only look at the progress she made from week to week with her teacher and stopped comparing herself with her friends. She still plays and even though she isn't a professional musician, she gets a lot of satisfaction out of it.

Despite the presence of comparative voices, we must remind ourselves that we have the right to dream, desire and try – and to enjoy our achievements – even if there are people who seemingly outperform us. By recognizing and minimizing the influence of comparative voices, we can focus on our own journey and personal growth.

THE VOICE OF FEAR

The voice of fear is often the most powerful of the three voices, and it's often the one we have the most trouble managing. This voice emerges when we confront our strengths, our ability to be who we aspire to be and our inner light. In moments when we feel like everything is possible, the voice of fear arrives as a powerful deterrent. Its role is to warn us of the consequences of embracing our true selves fully, without shame, concealment or apology.

The voice of fear can be paralyzing and immobilizing. It operates at critical moments, emerging at the precise instant of truth. It causes us to remain stagnant while opportunities pass us by and are sometimes taken by others.

I felt stopped by the voice of fear about 20 years ago, when I knew that my marriage was not working. I had thought about separating from my ex-wife, but I was too afraid to act upon my desire. I was constantly thinking about the consequences for my kids and what other people might say about my 'failure' to keep my family together.

But, underneath those concerns was another fear. I was afraid of the opportunity to live my life fully with passion, self-fulfillment and joy.

As a child, I was programmed to believe that life is hard and that you need to suffer on your way to achieve predetermined results, results that many people may not even want – like owning a house or having a successful career. Eventually, I got an external wakeup call. I was at a professional conference abroad and found myself feeling very lonely and sad. During the conference, I spent time with a woman who was both charming and beautiful, and I enjoyed her attention. Without much control over the situation, I fell for her. It shocked my whole being. When I went home and told my wife about it, everything exploded. It resulted in a very painful separation process in which everyone was hurt. I wish I could have recognized my fears earlier and seen them as an indication of the need to act. Had I done so, I would have made a change before being hijacked by an external force. That would have been better for myself, my ex-wife, my kids and everyone else that was involved.

The voice of fear is typically the hardest of the three to deal with. It is trying to protect us from the dramatic consequences of change. But if we know how to deal with it and can find ways to listen to what it has to tell us, we have the possibility of experiencing life-changing breakthroughs. The next two sections will describe how to do this.

GETTING ACQUAINTED WITH FEAR

When we stand on the edge of a cliff and look down, our body reacts with fear – the fear of falling. The same fear is present in our bodies before bungee jumping or skydiving. This is a good, functional fear that arises from our body to warn us and make us think carefully before taking hasty actions.

If we try to recall how this fear feels in terms of physical sensations, we might remember a rapid heartbeat, a cold sweat that chills the body, a feeling of paralysis or an urge to run away. These are survival mechanisms our body activates involuntarily to mobilize resources for the quickest and most effective escape.

However, there are situations where the danger is of a different nature. Try to imagine the last time you participated in a workshop or group meeting and, despite having something to say, you hesitated and felt intense inner turmoil. Or think about how you felt as you got ready to make a presentation to investors or speak in front of an audience. In these cases, the body often reacts with an accelerated heartbeat, sweat and a sensation of stress – functions of our body's sympathetic nervous system. However, the danger in these situations is not a real threat to life but rather a perceived threat arising from our thoughts, imagination and interpretation of the situation.

In modern life, there are many different sources of fear, ranging from physical situations to social and trauma-induced situations. Our body does not differentiate between these. In all of them, it activates our inner alarms – the 'fight or flight' response of the sympathetic nervous system.

The good news is that our **minds** can be trained to tell the difference between real threats and perceived threats. We can look at the fear-inducing situation and ask ourselves: Is this truly dangerous for me, or is it an instinctive response or a habit that could be reexamined? If the source of fear is mental and not physical, we can suspend the automatic instant response and make more conscious choices about situations in our lives that involve risk but are also part of a potential positive change. If we don't do this, then fear takes over and we will never make those changes.

I witnessed an example of how harnessing our inner strength can enable us to face challenges and grow personally and professionally through my coaching work with Shir, a senior manager at a software company. Shir had a very centralized style of leadership. Over time, she started to see the price she paid for this choice: she was burning out and the people who reported to her felt a lack of autonomy. In addition, the overall atmosphere of the company was lacking trust and creativity. Shir agreed to explore the possibility of delegating some of her responsibilities to other people in her team. This move wasn't easy for her, since she was afraid that work quality would be reduced, and she would not be able to control things the way she was used to. In other words, she was full of fear of failing. At one point in the process, Shir became ill and had to be away from work for ten days, making it hard for her to run things remotely as she had in similar situations in the past. She was surprised to see that some of the managers who reported to her kept projects running well. This event gave her the last push she needed to let go and count on her subordinates to rise to expectations. She made a conscious decision to walk through the fear with curiosity and courage to explore new opportunities for her as a leader.

MAKING FRIENDS WITH FEAR

By embracing fear as an invitation to explore new opportunities and unlock our hidden potential, we can learn to view it as a valuable ally on our journey toward self-discovery and personal growth. When we make friends with fear, we can allow it to guide us toward the treasure chest of our true selves, filled with unique qualities, talents and passions that make us who we are.

Omer, the senior executive who was so critical of himself and his employees, had to face his own inner fear of not being loved. As a child, the energy he spent to prove himself to his father was a survival mechanism. He believed that it kept him safe and, as a result, it became a rooted habit – to the point that he almost couldn't help but be critical of himself and of the world. To stop that pattern, he had to love, forgive and appreciate himself. He had to see that his felt experience was not a real danger but rather an imagined one. He had to stop and reassess the situation to realize that his fear was holding some future potential for him to change and become happier and more positive.

In the same manner, my daughter's fear that she would never play as well as her friends was be transformed into an inner knowing that her fear actually revealed something important for her: her vision of becoming a singer-songwriter. And finally, if I could have seen the fear of dissolving my marriage as a sign that there was a wide range of future possibilities that I could have explored instead of a fear that I should have been escaping from, then I might have navigated my transition more gracefully.

PERSONAL BALANCE

Beyond the voices of self-criticism, comparison and fear lies the realm of self-acceptance and unique personal presence. This is where we can access the jewels in our inner treasure chest and wear them without apologizing. In this state, we belong to ourselves and love ourselves as we are. We must be able to belong to ourselves before we can belong to any other group. This is not an easy task, and most people will work on it their entire life. But it is the foundation to healthy belonging.

One of the key aspects of finding balance in the paradox is the ability to be fully present in any given moment.

An athlete in the Olympic games who is moments away from her most important competition looks as if she is in the middle of an intense inner dialogue. This self-talk helps her quiet down the external distractions and focus her attention solely on her performance. In these moments, she is "in the zone," as is often said. She is deeply connected to her body, mind and soul, allowing her whole self to achieve the best possible results.

Being in the zone can be experienced by anyone in any field or activity, not just athletes. It is a state of heightened concentration in which one's skills and abilities are in harmony with the task at hand. This exceptional state allows individuals to perform at their highest potential, often surpassing their own expectations.

Developing the ability to enter the zone can lead to significant individual growth. It allows individuals to be more productive, creative and focused, ultimately contributing to a stronger sense of personal uniqueness and identity. But being in the zone requires you to be more than just an individual; it requires being part of a larger whole and belonging to something larger than you. This state has come to be called "being in the flow."

The concept of flow was developed by psychologist Mihaly Csikszentmihalyi in his book, *Flow*, to describe a state of optimal experience, peak performance and heightened creativity (Csikszentmihalyi 1991). Flow occurs when individuals are fully immersed in a task or situation. Their behavior is characterized by maximum concentration and a sense of effortless mastery. During flow, people often lose track of time, and their focus is entirely on the task at hand. They experience a sense of clarity. Their action is performed with ease and grace, thanks to the intense focus and turning off of external distractions.

Flow experiences are highly rewarding, and individuals often seek opportunities to recreate these moments, investing significant time and energy in the pursuit of flow states. We can find great examples of flow state in sports. One such example is Stephen Curry, a basketball player for the Golden State Warriors, whose flow-like state has made him one of the best shooters in the history of his sport. Curry makes his work seem effortless and ordinary. He is known for his pregame routines and exercises that engage the crowd and, in turn, energize him and enable him to access the flow state.

Other great examples of flow states can be found in the arts. Pablo Picasso's ability to work nonstop for days when he was engrossed in a project was described by his biographer John Richardson as being flow-like. Jimi Hendrix was said to often be lost in his guitar playing. He was renowned for his ability to be entirely in the moment during his performances.

Although the concept of flow might initially appear to be focused solely on an individual's personal experience, it also involves a connection to the environment, the world and nature. Flow can be considered a personal peak experience, but it goes beyond the self. Let's look at why.

Many people are familiar with Abraham Maslow's Hierarchy of Needs, which arranges fundamental and universal human needs into a pyramidal structure. Physiological needs, such as food and sleep, form the base of the pyramid, followed by safety and security, love and belonging, self-esteem, and finally self-actualization at the top.

However, few people are aware that later in his life, Maslow added a sixth level to his hierarchy: self-transcendence. He realized that peak experiences – moments of personal transcendence in which we are connected to the broader context of our lives – are of enormous importance. For this reason, he put them at the top of his pyramid, above self-actualization. Flow is self-transcendence.

In flow we transcend ourselves to become one with our relationships, with nature and with the world as a whole.

Self-transcendence can be achieved when we pursue something greater than ourselves. These pursuits include the connections we forge with others and the potential that arises from these relationships.

By combining the ideas of Mihaly Csikszentmihalyi's *Flow* and Abraham Maslow's self-transcendence, we can gain a deeper understanding of what it means to successfully navigate the Belonging Paradox: the ultimate human potential that emerges at the intersection of 'me' and 'we'. This is going to be explored in the next few chapters.

At the heart of embracing individuality lies the journey of recognizing our own worth and overcoming internal obstacles or limiting thoughts. Mastering the paradox at the individual level is about navigating the challenges of self-acceptance and realizing our potential while staying true to who we are. It's the foundation for being able to belong meaningfully within a group or community.

But our journey toward balancing the paradox doesn't end with ourselves – it extends into our relationships. In the next chapter, we will explore how balancing the paradox takes shape in our closest bonds. Whether it's friendships, romantic partnerships or the relationships we have with our children, we will see how maintaining our individuality while deeply connecting with others forms the basis of healthy and fulfilling relationships.

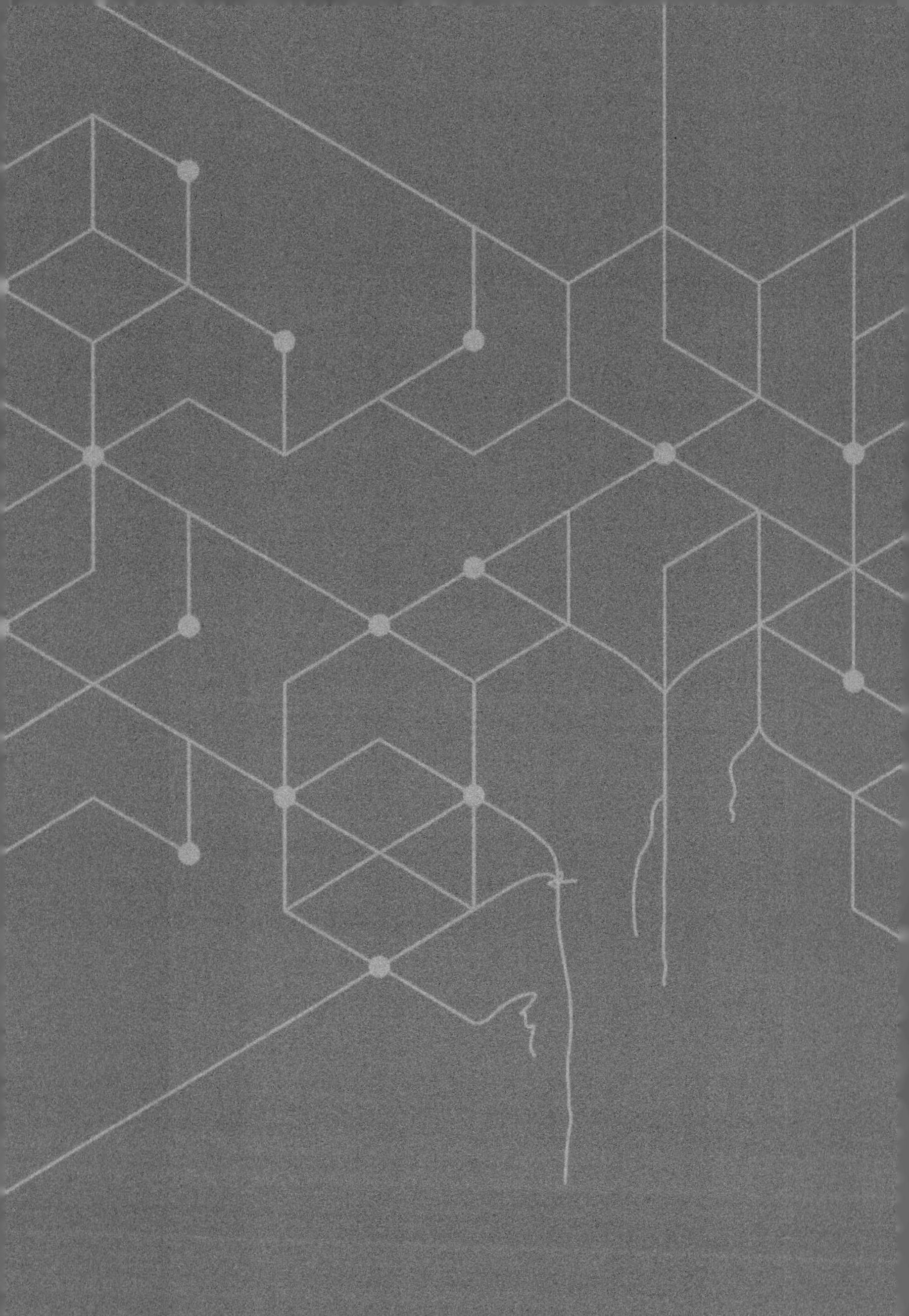

CHAPTER 6

BALANCING THE PARADOX IN RELATIONSHIPS WITH CLOSE PEOPLE

FRIENDSHIP

Reflect on the people you consider your closest friends, those with whom you've managed to nurture relationships over the years. At the heart of these connections lies the success in mastering the Belonging Paradox – a harmonious blend of individuality and belonging.

My bond with my friend Eli perfectly encapsulates the essence of this. We met in a professional setting: I was the team-building facilitator for a week-long retreat, and Eli was the spirited outdoor training provider. While our personalities differed – Eli, charismatic and charming with youthful zest, and I, grounded, focused and visionary – it was these very differences that, when we were together, became our strength.

This synergy propelled us to cofound the Impact Hub in Tel Aviv, an incubator for social entrepreneurs that was part of a global chain of such spaces. In this venture, I delved into business development, carefully planning our growth trajectory. Eli, with his undeniable charisma, became the heartbeat of the place, ensuring every visitor felt not just welcomed, but truly seen and valued. Our local Impact Hub birthed 30 companies and served 300 entrepreneurs in fulfilling their dreams. Our co-parenting of The-Hub was one of the first things people noticed when they visited: a co-hosted space that allowed the conception and birth of people's creativity and innovative ventures. This was only possible thanks to the balance each of us kept between our unique presence and our oneness as friends and partners.

While our shared enterprise faced its share of challenges over the five years we ran it, our foundational bond, steeped in mutual respect and shared vision, remained unshaken. When the time came and we had to close our shared venture, it was with deep compassion and understanding for each other's unfulfilled goals and dreams. Our journey reflected the enduring strength of friendships rooted in the principles of mastering the Belonging Paradox.

True friends accept us as we are, with all our nuances. We belong to the same friendship unit of two or more. Even when conflicts arise, they are resolved through deep love and mutual acceptance. Genuine friendship is like a mixed salad of human experiences: you love, hate, hurt, forgive, fall and rise, all while remaining authentic and without façades.

However, not all enduring relationships embody this golden balance. Some continue despite underlying strains of exploitation, dependency or inequality. Such relationships might tick the time box but often lack genuine happiness and sense of belonging. When a relationship dims your spirit, rather than elevating it, the Belonging Paradox is not well balanced.

With the Belonging Paradox concept in mind, it might be easier to audit our friendships: Is it an effort to hold a friendship? Is it one-sided? Do you feel authentic and yourself in this friendship? Can you be vulnerable? Can you count on your friends to be there for you when you really need them? Is it love or fear that drives the connection? Answering these questions can lead to some painful conclusions but may also help to move on and open doors to more fulfilling relationships that truly resonate with our sense of self and the core values. Mastering the Belonging Paradox can lead to a more authentic and rewarding social circle.

COUPLES

This understanding extends to couples and life partners as well.

I have this tendency, which I think is rooted in human biology, to scan every new space I enter and immediately identify the most attractive potential partners. This is exactly what I did that morning in 2008 when I stepped into the domestic-flights terminal in Tel Aviv. I saw Rachel standing there, beautiful and mysterious, and I noted to myself that she was interesting. It was not by chance that I stood beside her in the queue to the bus that took us to the plane. She noticed me and asked: "Are you also going to the university campus?" I wasn't going to the same destination, but it was enough to start a conversation. We weren't seated near each other on the plane, but I was brave enough to approach her after the landing and give her my business card inviting her to call me when she felt like meeting for a coffee. The same evening, when both of us were back from work, she called. We met and it was the start of a passionate and exhilarating relationship.

As with my story with Rachel most of the inceptions of relationships are often marked by a thrilling romantic narrative. Whether it is a serendipitous encounter or a planned match, those who have fallen in love can attest to the elating period when hearts are fully devoted to each other, with thoughts consumed by love. This intense phase can last several months or even, in rare cases, years.

However, as time passes, the passion and all-consuming emotions tend to wane, giving way to a relationship grounded in friendship, shared interests, joint aspirations and sometimes family life. This shift is a natural progression in all romantic relationships, as the energy levels of the initial 'falling in love' phase are too high to maintain indefinitely.

In the years following this stage, the delicate balance between individuality and partnership comes into focus. In a balanced relationship, each partner continues to grow and mature, learning, working, socializing and having unique experiences. Simultaneously, the couple as a unit evolves, gathering shared experiences, assets, mutual friends and sometimes shared children. In the ideal world, both partners feel supported for their personal aspirations and dreams. It doesn't always have to be at the same time. Partners may take turns stepping up and backing up (i.e., "This year I will back you up while you take this demanding job. When you feel you have reached stability, I will start my own company") but the overall equation should be balanced.

This dynamic isn't always easy to maintain. For this reason, it is within this dynamic that we often see examples of partnerships that aren't healthy. Some couples tend to overlook the individuality of each partner, engaging in activities together, often working side-by-side, thinking in unison and consistently using 'we' language. They prioritize shared experiences, spend all their free time together and communicate constantly, even when physically apart. You might even find them using a joint email address or sharing a couple's Facebook profile and calling each other seven or eight times a day. From the outside, these couples may appear harmonious and idyllic. However, the individuality of each partner becomes somewhat stifled. Moreover, one or both of the partners can become obsessed with preserving the unity and hence limiting the freedom of the other side so that there will be no danger to the tight connection.

If this pattern persists for many years, what began as a pause in individual growth and freedom may turn into neglect. The need for unique and personal development is innate and, if left unfulfilled, it can foster inner resentment and frustration. In the early stages, these feelings might be suppressed, brewing behind the main 'show' of the seemingly perfect couple. But over time, frustration accumulates to an unbearable level, ultimately leading to a crisis.

My parents were an old-fashioned couple who stayed together despite all the turmoil and fights between them. I remember as a child thinking, "Why on earth should they stay together and continue this ongoing pain?" Most of the time I identified with my mom's side especially because she seemed weaker and suffered from my father's anger bursts, though she wasn't fully passive and returned her portion of rage and resentment. I am sure there was also love and respect between them, but I couldn't see that as a child. In a retrospect, I now understand that my mom had to put aside her own dreams and aspirations to support my father. She stepped back and raised my brother and me while my father climbed up the ladder of his medical career. I am sure she wasn't less talented or capable than him and that she could succeed as much as he did. A small indication of this assumption is that they both loved to play cards. He used to play bridge (a strategic and sophisticated cards game) with his male friends, while she had to settle with playing rummy (a more straightforward and easy cards game) with the female spouses. But her true aspiration was to learn bridge and excel in it. Slowly, under the radar, she started to learn bridge and go to competitions where he and his gang were always at the top. She started to outperform them and win prizes that left them behind. When my father realized the new situation, he changed his attitude toward her and invited her to be his formal partner at these competitions. They won a lot of trophies together and it was her small revenge. But that was the exception. Generally, she didn't claim her place and stayed in his shadow. He, in turn, made all the efforts to provide the family with the resources needed to make sure that we didn't lack anything in our typical middle-class, modest family. But these dreams and aspirations that my mom gave up never disappeared. They just transformed into resentment and made her a heavy smoker despite the fact that she was diagnosed with breast cancer and was advised to stop. She never stopped. Smoking was her ultimate rebellion and claim for freedom within the constraints of her marriage. While this is a typical story that didn't break them as a couple, it is not a great example of mastering the Belonging Paradox.

An ongoing conflict between couples that is occurring due to lack of balance may manifest in various ways: a dramatic explosion accompanied by feelings of betrayal, or more moderate discussions and negotiations. Sometimes, the crisis prompts a reevaluation of the couple's initial psychological (often unspoken) agreement and the needs of each individual within the partnership. In other cases, it results in separation. Regardless, the imbalance and neglect of individuality in the couple create an intolerable situation.

It becomes inevitable that one or both partners will need to address and resolve the issue.

A lack of Belonging Paradox balance in a couple's life can also stem from a different source. After the initial passion subsides, the couple may settle into a comfort zone where the relationship appears to be 'working well'. Within this comfort zone, each partner focuses on personal growth, pursuing unique interests that may not resonate with the other. Initially, this arrangement might suit both partners, as they view it as a testament to the freedom and flexibility they grant one another. However, if the couple neglects to invest in creating shared experiences and cultivating common interests, the relationship can gradually devolve into one resembling that of roommates or business partners. They may manage their affairs separately but lack the deeper emotional connection necessary for maintaining the friendship that is so much needed for maintaining a nourishing relationship.

To nurture a sense of belonging balance, it is essential for couples to strike a balance between individual pursuits and shared experiences that deepen their emotional connection. This is easier said than done. To achieve that, it is important to understand the psychological mechanism behind our bonds and ongoing relationship with a specific partner.

Intimate relationships hold great potential for healing trauma and emotional wounds. Each individual in a partnership carries a unique set of emotional scars and traumas from their childhood and adolescence, which have left lasting impressions. As they transition from adolescence to early adulthood (ages 20–30), people often learn to accept themselves and discover ways to express their identity in the world. Many begin to heal from the traumas experienced during adolescence and mature into independent, whole individuals who are ready to engage in meaningful relationships.

Upon entering a relationship, these seemingly healed traumas may start to resurface. This occurs because the intimacy of a close relationship can recreate the conditions in which these traumas were initially formed. Traumas often involve significant people in our lives, and without a deep connection with someone, these emotional wounds can remain dormant. When we encounter a significant partner, it can awaken these dormant traumas, compelling us to face old patterns once again.

In an intimate relationship, the reenactment of the trauma occurs first as emotional scars playing like video clips on a loop within a person's mental system. In a relationship, one partner acts as a movie projector, replaying these painful clips repeatedly. The other partner, in turn, serves as a blank screen onto which these videos are projected. In doing so, one person in the relationship projects their negative memories onto the other, casting them in the role of the villain and generating a reenacting conflict. For example, I have some mental scars burnt into my unconscious operating system from witnessing as a child the fights and struggles between my parents. I believe that somehow the pattern of blaming that my father had toward my mother is rooted in my own behavioral repertoire. So, too often I find myself blaming Rachel, my partner, for things that I see in her behavior (especially in the work of raising our children). I find it hard to take responsibility for my own part in the events. In that sense, I project on her my tendency to blame. It would probably happen with every other partner, and it is something I must own and heal if I want to find a constructive path.

Initially, the other person may not fully comprehend why they are entangled in this conflict and might assume it is somehow related to them. As the pattern repeats itself, conflicts emerge, and the situation turns into a self-fulfilling prophecy. The individual onto whom the trauma is projected starts reacting with impatience and hurt toward the projecting partner. The projecting partner, conversely, receives validation that their traumas are still 'active' and becomes entrenched in a blaming or victim mentality. This dynamic typically occurs in both directions, with both partners acting as projectors and screens, further intensifying the conflict.

In my own story, luckily, Rachel is not only a great partner but also a wise mentor. She consistently shows me that my projections at her are only part of the story. She insists that I take responsibility for my part as well. When she does that I don't always like it. But since she has the wisdom of doing it gently and with patience, it helps me take more responsibility on my own issues and start to heal, hence stop projecting at her my own issues.

With every reenactment of past traumas, there is also an opportunity for a healing phase. Emotionally intelligent and self-aware couples intuitively recognize that recurring conflicts that may seem casual, arise and escalate due to past traumas. In such instances, they must learn how to soothe each other, take breaks and avoid becoming entrenched in the argument. The ability to pause an automatic reaction and prevent conflict contains the potential for profound healing. Each partner should learn that past traumas don't have to dictate the present, and pain can be met with a receptive, understanding and supportive partner. In this manner, the trauma gradually weakens until it eventually dissipates. A healthy relationship serves as the optimal remedy for healing past traumas.

Unfortunately, in many cases, the emotional intelligence needed for the scenario described above is not easily accessible. We are not taught these tools as children at school and typically the only model that we have to learn from is our family, which is not always the best place to learn from. Therefore, many conflicts that couples experience that stem from past traumas accumulate and become an obstacle that makes the lives of the partners miserable. This is where experienced couples therapists can really help. Their work is to help each individual in the couple to be more aware of their own shadows and how they project them onto the other side. At the same time, they help the other side not be offended by the projection and support their partner in their healing process.

The mechanism depicted here, of reenactment with healing, embodies mastering the Belonging Paradox at its finest. Each individual in the relationship brings their own unique story and the way it shaped their virtues as well as their triggers and patterns. If the couple succeeds in hosting each other in a supportive and nourishing manner it creates the strongest and most healthy partnership, hence a belonging that is based on embracing each other's uniqueness. If not, it can lead to a destructive relationship that amplifies pain and sorrow. Psychological resilience develops from confronting difficulties and conflicts, rather than avoiding or suppressing them. A meaningful relationship cannot remain healthy if each partner suppresses their story due to fear of causing conflict. The unique journey of a couple is full of conflicts and resolutions. Couples who navigate this journey and remain together can write volumes on conflict resolution, listening, empathy, compromise, sacrifice and ultimately, healing and recovery. Mastering the Belonging Paradox in couples' relationships is an ongoing dynamic process that demands a lot of hard work and faith.

PARENT-CHILD RELATIONSHIPS

Parenthood is type of relationship that involves the deepest levels of love as well as the deepest fears and worries. Anyone who has experienced raising children can recall the roller-coaster of emotions.

My eldest daughter is a great example of this stormy journey. She was a beautiful child, her long blond hair falling gracefully over her shoulders, framing her expressive blue eyes. Possessing a natural creativity, she was always busy writing stories, inventing games and creating art. She loved pets and was very knowledgeable in everything regarding animals and zoological facts.

At age ten, she started the weird behavior of pulling her scalp hair, which was so destructive and painful to watch.

Later we understood it was a hair-pulling disorder called trichotillomania. We tried to stop her from pulling hair, to film her behavior and show it to her, to speak with her about the meaning of it, but nothing helped. It reached a point where she was completely bald. She started to wear kerchiefs and people looked at her and at me with pity as if they knew she was suffering from cancer. It was a nightmare. The disorder was extremely difficult to treat, causing immense pain and hardship for both her and our family. Despite our efforts and various treatments, we were unable to find a solution that worked for her. My frustration grew as I struggled to help my daughter, and I felt helpless.

One day, when she was around 16, she was sitting on the sofa in the living room, busy writing one of her original stories, and pulling her hair as a regular, unconscious routine. I was standing there, watching her as always, with so much pain, knowing that I could say nothing because it would just make her more upset and wouldn't change anything. So, I was just staring and reflecting. At a certain point she noticed me staring at her. This led to a wild outpouring of emotions from her, as she yelled, "Why are you always giving me this judgmental stare? When will you finally accept me for who I am? Why don't you just accept me as your daughter with my tendency to pull my hair out? Just accept me!" I was shocked. She was right. I did judge her, and it was obviously noticeable.

This moment was a turning point for me. I realized that my own misery was projected as judgment toward her and that this had caused her immense pain and suffering. I realized that although I really wanted the best for her

I was doing the opposite. By showing her my critical face and by not accepting her with her flaws I was weakening her and making her more miserable because she had to both deal with her symptoms as well as with an unhappy and judgmental father. I had to find a way to accept her and stop judging. It wasn't easy. Judging and being critical is part of my automatic behaviors. I have dreams and expectations for my children and when things don't go well according to my plans I feel pain. I had to learn to let go of my expectations and see my child as a separate entity that was beautiful in its own way. I had to learn to stop the unconscious pattern of turning disappointment into judgment. My daughter's reaction felt like a slap in my face, which ironically helped me get out of my bubble and stop my critical and worried presence. My own process allowed my daughter to continue her own journey with one less thing to worry about.

The solution came about completely her own way, creatively invented and powered by her unique imagination. As a child she was always busy with online computer games, and she loved recording her screen while playing and posting it on YouTube. She only had a few friends following her video clips, but it didn't bother her. She was inspired by other YouTube influencers who did the same and had many more followers. Gradually she gained more confidence in the YouTube platform and started a channel on which she was filming herself telling other girls about her life struggles and joys. She started to gain more and more attention and the numbers of followers started to climb. There was something authentic in her voice that girls adored. The need to stand in front of a camera made her more aware and responsible for how she looked. She started to grow her hair again. But this time she also added crazy color dyeing. It was quite unusual at the time and made her stand out and she was considered very original and authentic. She became a hit. Over a period of a few months, she became one of the most popular influencers in Israel, with an audience of more than 150,000. She became known for her beautifully colored long hair and that became her unique signature. She also added a lot of colorful fashion to her look and became one of the top-rated fashionistas in Israel. It was all her own invention and came from a place of accepting herself, flaws and all. Once that happened, she became a superstar and felt the joy of belonging and love. I made a very small contribution to this miracle when I embraced her for who she truly was – and that was exactly what she needed from me in order to proceed with her own journey.

FAMILY: WHERE BELONGING STARTS

The family serves as the primary location where the meaning of 'we' is first experienced. This is where we first learn to belong and, simultaneously, where our individuality as separate, unique beings also takes shape.

Typically, we are born into a family in which we gradually learn that we are part of a larger system. In well-functioning families, this system attends to our needs and helps us grow. As we grow, we have to be aware of the other family members' needs as well as the needs of the family as a unit. In well-functioning families, there exists a harmonious balance between the 'me' and 'we'. In an ideal situation, each member is granted the opportunity to explore and cultivate their own sense of self, beyond the constraints of their family expectations or social norms, an exploration that spans a lifetime. In the early stages of this quest, the family may support the child in developing a sense of choice and inner freedom, allowing for exploration and shaping of the self-identity and narrative.

Unfortunately, there are dysfunctional sides to many families around the world. Conflicts between parents that impact children and ineffective methods of resolving conflicts are among the typical problems. One of the common complaints that children voice when reflecting on their upbringing within the family is "I wasn't seen, I wasn't heard." My conflict with my daughter had an element of this, as became apparent to me, when she screamed, "Just accept me!" This widespread issue stems from multiple reasons. First, in many family environments globally, parents are occupied with earning a living, making them less accessible and available to their children. This distance can be perceived as "they don't see me." However, a more pressing reason is often the parents' expectations of their children. All too often, decisions are made for the children based on the belief that the parents know what is best for them. This is exactly where I was when I tried to change my daughter and didn't accept her with the disorder she had. I tried to 'fix' her because of my expectations. There are instances where making decisions for children is appropriate. For example, when a child wishes to continue watching screens at night and the parent realizes that it is better for the child to sleep, the intervention of the parent is reasonable. On the other hand, if the parents decide that the child must become a doctor because they are capable and carry the family's hopes and expectations, despite the child's aversion to anything related to medicine, this constitutes an excessive intervention born from not seeing the child's real needs and interests.

Many children grow up under such pressure of expectations. Sometimes the child receives this pressure positively, but more often children feel suffocated and trapped. In extreme cases, children retreat into themselves out of the belief that no one listens to them or hears their needs. This leads to a cycle of frustration as the parents, eager for communication, increase the pressure, causing the children to shut down even further. Children who don't experience a balanced 'we' or 'us' in their families go into the world with a deficiency of attention and trust.

Parents who raise children with physical or mental disabilities often develop a unique sensitivity and understanding. It is always moving to hear parents of children with autism speak about their child with great love and affection, referring to them as "the greatest gift of our lives." These children challenge their parents to abandon preconceived notions of 'right' and 'necessary' and to truly open themselves up to their child's unique needs. Through this process, these special children teach their parents a more connected and empathetic form of parenting, encouraging them to listen to the depths of their child's needs rather than adhering to their own preconceptions.

In a similar vein, special education schools often lead the way in educational advancements because of the ways in which they have to reinvent teaching as a much more adaptable and attentive practice. They lead the way in creating differentiated learning that suits each student's learning style, they lead in creating innovative technologies to overcome learning disabilities, and they lead in making the best education accessible and inclusive for all. If one wishes to revolutionize the education system, they should look to these institutions for guidance on how to best support and educate children with special needs and create a sense of uniqueness and belonging at the same time.

Each child is born with a unique set of traits, tendencies and talents, and they require support, love and recognition for who they are. However, there is a delicate balance between providing these things and overstepping boundaries, which can stifle a child's growth and limit their freedom to develop. Parenting is a complex art, but it has the power to raise children who are truly one-of-a-kind and cultivate a strong and united family bond.

In our closest relationships – whether with friends, romantic partners, or family members – balancing individuality and togetherness is key. The journey of cultivating this balance allows for growth, healing and deeper connection. But this same balancing act doesn't end at home; it extends into every group and community we become a part of.

Belonging is a core human need, but it presents its own set of challenges. In the next chapter, we will explore the tension between maintaining our individuality and the desire for acceptance in larger social groups. As we delve into the psychology of belonging, we'll see why it's often difficult to find a healthy balance and how our ego plays a crucial role in shaping how we navigate this complex dynamic.

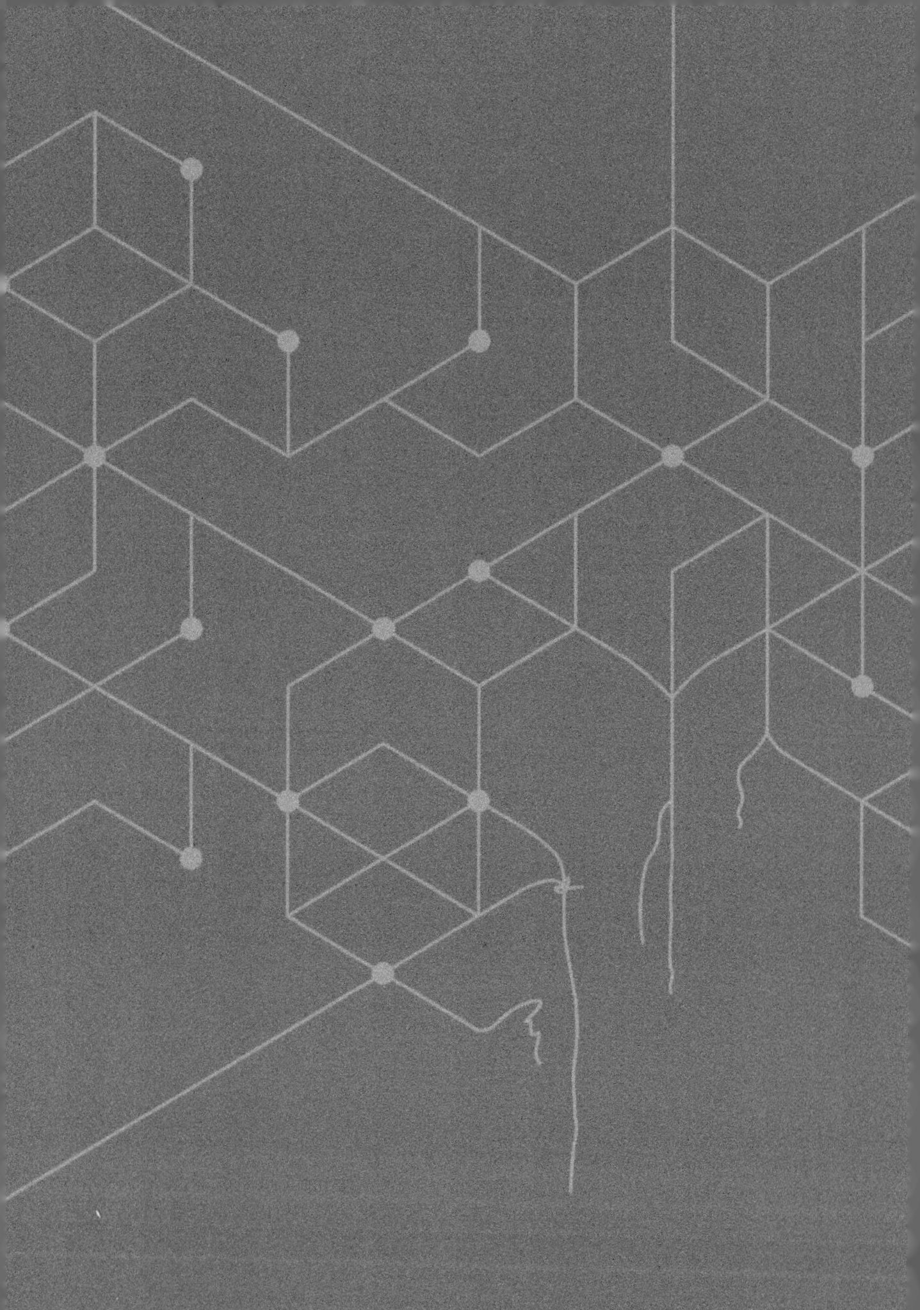

CHAPTER 7

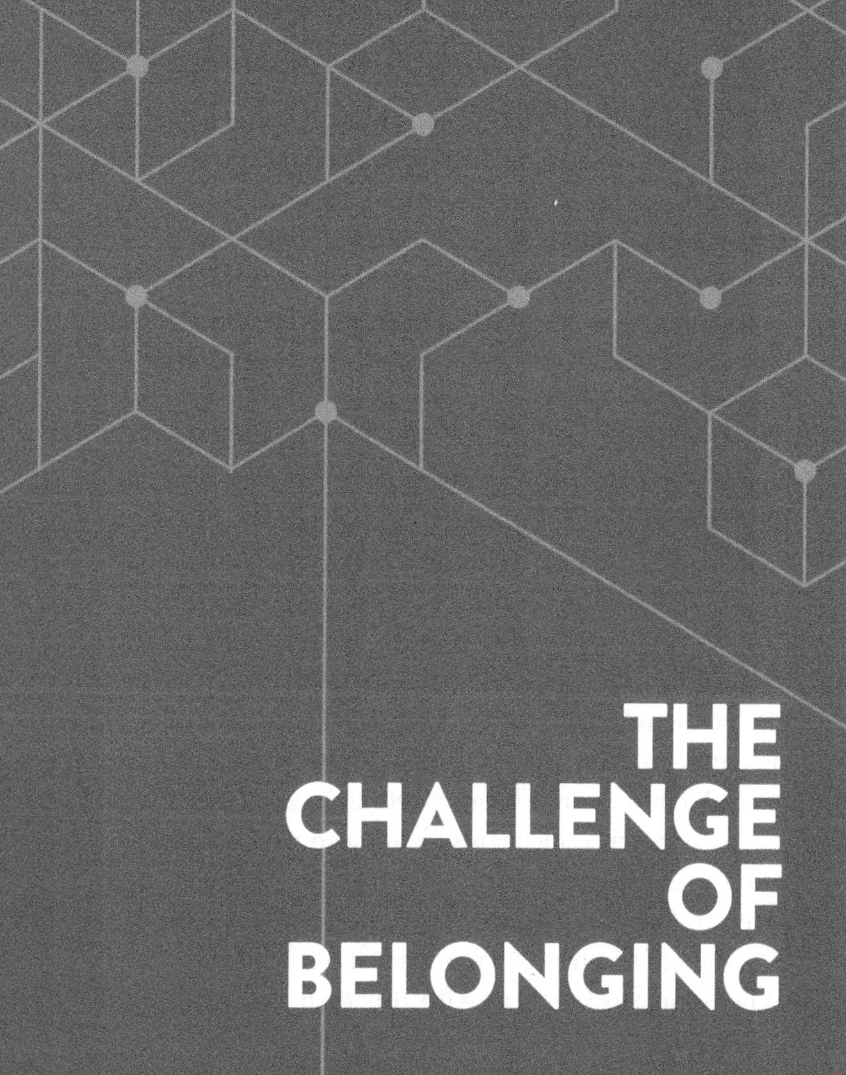

THE CHALLENGE OF BELONGING

"I refuse to join any club that would have me as a member" is a quote attributed to Groucho Marx, a renowned American comedian and film star. I love this quote with its bittersweet paradox. It captures the desire to be accepted while feeling critical toward any group that would be willing to accept someone like oneself. It speaks to the heart of the challenge of belonging: the tension between individuality and social acceptance.

While being a born tendency rooted in our nature as humans, belonging is not an easy task. It puts some serious challenges, mainly to our ego, that make us hesitate before taking a step and signing in. According to Freud, the ego is one of the three basic elements of our personality. The other two are the **id**, which is responsible for the immediate satisfaction of our needs, and the **superego**, which is responsible for the moral-societal norms, which are often delivered to us by our parents and other significant others as part of our upbringing. The **ego**'s function is, according to Freud, an important mediating mechanism that represents reality within this tension between the instinctual desires and the moral norms. As such, the ego is a very hard-working mechanism that has to constantly balance us and keep our legs on the ground. To maintain balance, the ego employes a set of defense mechanisms such as denial, regression and projection. These mechanisms are crucial to keep us in a balanced state.

These defense mechanisms are also used to navigate our relationships with other people's egos, which may interpret reality differently from our own. From the earliest days of life, this dynamic shapes our social existence. When our ego interacts with others, it can spark love, hate and a wide range of human experiences, both good and bad. This interaction is at the heart of belonging, as well as the challenges that come with it.

When facing external interactions, our ego employs defense mechanisms that shape our behaviors and influence relationship dynamics. Take projection, for example: this mechanism involves attributing one's own unacceptable thoughts, feelings or insecurities to someone else. For instance, a person with low self-esteem might accuse another of being insecure or incompetent. In doing so, the ego reduces internal stress and preserves inner peace, but it can also affect the other person, who may perceive this as either a threat or an invitation. The response from the other side depends on that perception, which can lead to either connection or exclusion.

Our ego often feels hurt or defensive when encountering others who see the world differently. Why? Because the ego is so focused on being 'right' that it fails to recognize that the other side may also be right. This is why interactions often feel unfair to our ego, which then overuses defense mechanisms to protect us.

Understanding ego theory helps us see why being part of a group can feel risky. It forces you out of your 'cave' and into the light, where you're visible to others, making you vulnerable to evaluation, judgment or gossip. For some, this exposure can trigger memories of past painful experiences, such as feeling rejected or mistreated in a group setting.

On a personal note, I faced a dilemma while writing this book: should I write it in Hebrew, my mother tongue, where I feel most at home, or in English, the language that would allow me to reach a global audience? While Hebrew is the language I naturally express myself in, I felt a strong desire to share these ideas beyond the borders of Israel, where the themes of belonging, empathy and human connection resonate and can have a broader impact.

Choosing English wasn't just about reaching more people – it was about inviting a wider community into the conversation. However, as I reflected on my choice, I realized there were deeper, more personal reasons at play. Writing in Hebrew would have placed me under the judgment of my Israeli colleagues, and I found myself seeking the freedom to express my thoughts without that concern. This realization reminded me of my own hesitations and fears about belonging, much like in Groucho Marx's famous quote.

My story is also the story of my children who struggled in their quest for acceptance and being popular or at least not marginalized. My older daughter, for instance, started her social quest in her first daycare when she was only nine months old. She was late to walk by herself, while most of the children were already walking. So, she had to crawl her way to toys or other activities while her friends outpaced her. She was also put in a group with younger babies when her same-age friends had an activity that demanded sitting and walking. I believe, even at such a young age, her ego made her feel inferior and out of the group. Later when she was in kindergarten she used to tell us that she had no friends and that she felt alone. When we spoke to the teacher she said that on the contrary, our daughter was very much loved by her friends and had so many good interactions during the day. We knew that the truth lay somewhere in between. She was very friendly and creative in making friends and finding her way to what she desired, but at the same time she was very sensitive to any behavior that seemed like exclusion, and when those happened she tended to interpret them as such and get hurt. This hypersensitivity was the other side of her friendliness. She was very good at sensing social situations and finding ways to be part of the game, but if something didn't go according to her plans, she was very easily offended and gave the situation an interpretation of exclusion.

This story isn't unique to my family alone. Many people experience the mixed feelings of wanting to belong but fearing rejection, judgement or an unpleasant feeling of not fitting in. To be more successful in fitting-in and belonging people need to be less sensitive and less bothered by regular group dynamics that don't match their preferences or expectations. One option is to become a little numb and less occupied with external dynamics. But this option may be a little counterproductive in a group setting since to fit in one must also be aware of others' needs and positions. But if we don't become numb and keep our natural senses open, we become aware of the needs of other egos around us and that can cause tension or even conflict. Our ego guides us to hold expectations about how things should work. We are constantly busy with how we are doing in light of these expectations. Often, these expectations are not met. This is troubling and doesn't allow us to fit in. If we want to increase our ability to belong we need to train our ego to loosen the grip of the expectations. Less attachment to our expectations will allow us to relax and calmly accept everything that may happen.

Loosening our ego's tendency to protect us and hold on to expectations is not an easy task. Not only because it is an old habit that was formed in the early days of our personal development, but also because it is part of who we are, it defines our self-perception that is often called 'self' or 'I.' People are not easily ready to let go of something that defines them. We need stability in the way we perceive ourselves, and that provides us with a sense of safety. We believe that our 'self' is part of our unique human signature, which in the context of our discussion here may be important for keeping the balance of the Belonging Paradox. In that case, we should ask whether letting go of our perceived self necessarily means letting go of our uniqueness. I believe not.

In the beginning of our lives, as explained earlier, the ego is an important entity that protects us by balancing the conflict between our instinctual desires and the moral voices of society ("you should," "you shouldn't"). The ego also protects us from other egos and the threat of being hurt by them. This is done by unconscious defense mechanisms. As we grow up we become more aware of our interpersonal dynamics and how they activate our internal defenses. We gradually learn to be more in control of our instinctual desires and the external moral voices. Therefore, there may be less need for the protection of the ego with its arsenal of defense mechanisms. However, many individuals find that their ego, shaped by early experiences, continues to employ these defense mechanisms even when the original threats are no longer present. This habitual response can obscure our true selves by creating a false sense of self that is the sum of our defense mechanisms.

It blocks the development of parts of the self that are really unique and not just a way to defend ourselves. So, by letting go of these defense mechanisms, we are actually increasing the ability to grow our authentic self and focus on its uniqueness rather than what it is not. Therefore, the movement toward letting go of ego-power is actually positively contributing to our ability to practice belonging that balances the authentic self with the natural tendency and longing to be part of a social group.

The ability to belong in a healthy way is crucial for our social life. It helps us be able to become members of a community. A community is maybe the oldest social structure in nature. Since the dawn of humanity people formed communities to provide security and protection from threats they couldn't face alone. The first communities were place-based. But over time as people started to travel, they found other commonalities that allowed them to organize around topics beyond geography, like shared interest, activism, hobbies and life circumstances.

Communities don't last forever. What keeps them alive are two conditions: the first is the reason for the forming, the why, the meaning. The second is group dynamics. The first is like a magnet and glue that holds everyone together from the beginning. The latter is what makes people feel (or lack) a sense of belonging. A community is based on different levels of participation. It must have a core of community holders who take it as their duty to keep the flame on. Then there is another circle of people who are involved and active. And there is another circle of people who are interested and attend. And then there is another circle of people who support it but stay relatively passive.

The community usually has some tolerance for the diversity of involvement levels. A positive dynamic is when each member feels that they are accepted for who they are, respected and invited to participate without judgement. When this works well the community provides each unique individual with a precious sense of belonging. In such cases the community can last even if the initial reason for its forming has changed.

Sometimes a community crosses an important threshold. This happens when there is a demand from the core leadership of the community to let go of one's own uniqueness and to fully be devoted or surrender to the charismatic leader. There is a fine line between a community and a sect. At the beginning, it looks like a very attractive place that is welcoming you and appreciates you, but slowly it starts to demand that you get rid of any individuality and start worshipping the leader. There is no place for your uniqueness in a sect and, therefore, it is as far as possible from a balanced belonging. A good way to know if your community is a sect is to express yourself and see the reaction. A sect will not tolerate individual expression, and it is a good sign that you should consider your next steps.

Communities are an important part of our adult life, where we spend a lot of time. But many of us spend a great part of our adult time at a special kind of community known as 'work'. As we move from exploring the challenges of belonging in social and community contexts to considering the world of work, we must ask ourselves: Do organizations support our human need for belonging while also respecting our individuality? In the next chapter, we will delve into the complex relationship we have with the places where we spend a significant portion of our adult lives: our workplaces. Are organizations truly good for people? Let's examine how these environments shape our sense of belonging and impact our wellbeing.

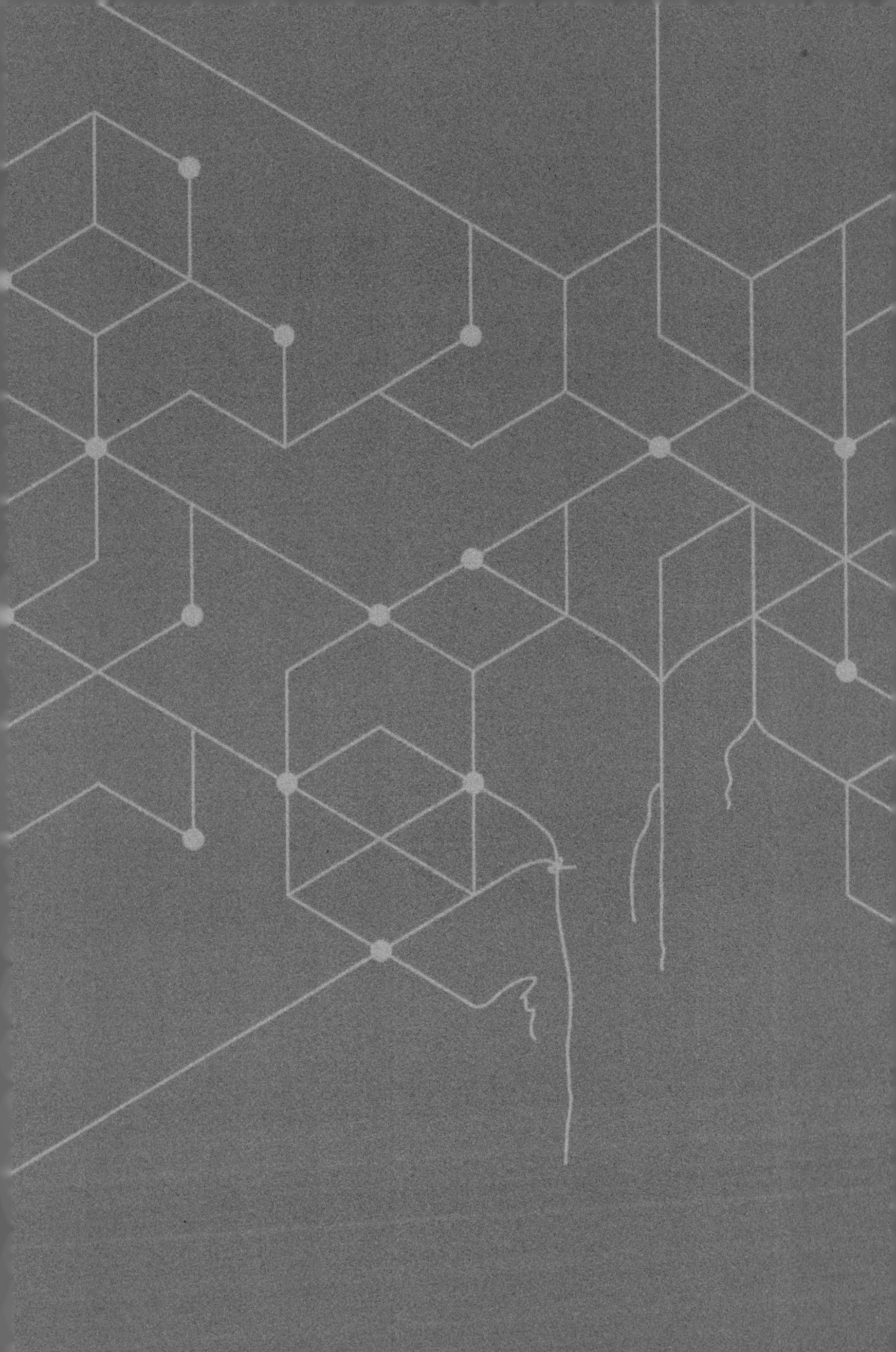

CHAPTER 8

ARE ORGANIZATIONS GOOD FOR PEOPLE?

As adults, we dedicate a significant portion of our lives to work. Would we make the same choice if given an alternative? A 2023 global Gallup survey reveals that only 23% of workers worldwide feel engaged with their jobs. In Europe, this figure falls below the global average, with a mere 13% of workers feeling engaged, while in North America, the engagement rate is higher at 31%. Regardless of location and culture, these figures are disturbingly low and trigger a critical inquiry: Do workplaces contribute positively to people's lives? Are individuals excited about going to work, or is it merely a necessity driven by the need to earn a living? These questions deserve our attention. The reality is that most adults worldwide report to their jobs daily. Would they still do so if financial constraints were not a concern?

My relationship with the world of organizations is a love-hate affair. On one hand, my profession and career as an organizational consultant, where I gained a lot of satisfaction and self-fulfillment, are entirely based on the organizational world. On the other hand, as someone who has studied organizations and observed them under a magnifying glass for many years, I can see why so many employees don't feel engaged in their workplaces. I see a lot of people who start their jobs with a lot of motivation, wishing to excel and meet the expectations of those who hired them. Gradually, this enthusiasm erodes – often because of managers who don't listen, toxic cultures and lack of psychological safety. Younger children who face such circumstances would probably seek help from their parents or the school counselor, or just quit. But as adults, we feel the need to be tough and that we should hide our vulnerability. Organizational life always involves both positive challenges of growth and development as well as tensions and conflicts that result in hurt or disappointment. If hurt is accumulated internally, without a proper outlet, it becomes frustration and eventually leads to lack of engagement and daydreams of quitting. The Gallup engagement statistics show that people at large are not happy in organizations despite the fact they must go there every day.

THE COMPLEX REALITY OF WORKING IN ORGANIZATIONS

The relationship we have with our work is complicated, filled with both satisfaction and frustration. On the one hand, our jobs give us something to wake up for – they allow us to provide for our families, introduce us to new friends and challenge us to grow. But on the other hand, we often feel like mere instruments used to achieve organizational goals rather than as human beings that have unique contributions and life beyond work. The pressure to meet targets and please higher-ups can be overwhelming, especially when our hard work is not always recognized or acknowledged. Often, we face conflicting demands that challenge our personal values, or struggle to understand strategic directions that seem disconnected from our reality. This confusion and discouragement erodes our initial passion, and we start to lose sight of why we bother to wake up each morning to pour

our energy into something that doesn't truly resonate with who we are.

This delicate balance between needing our jobs and wrestling with the discomfort they bring shows just how complex our relationship with work can be – it's something that sustains us, yet at times, can also drain us. The people in organizations are me, you, us: good people full of good intentions. So, how is it that we are not so successful in creating organizations that are good for us? One could even expand this question and ask: How can human history be full of organizations, including countries, armies and corporations, that were full of people with good intentions but still caused institutional and structural damage to the planet and humanity? There is no simple answer, but it often starts when ordinary people with good intentions are lost in the maze of organizational life.

THE SCALING-UP CHALLENGE

I have seen in my consulting work many startups that began as cohesive groups of dedicated people ready to do everything for their dream, only to evolve into larger companies where engagement dropped and turnover raised, damaging both business and culture.

One example is a large global tech company that started with just two friends in a small apartment. Like in the startups' typical story, they worked day and night to develop the initial product that raised the interest of some investors and gained an initial investment. The days of the startup phase were characterized by deep friendship, trust, mutual care and shared destiny. They developed their own way of doing things, an unspoken language that helped them to crack any technological or business challenge. As they grew, they hired new people who brought different ideas and values. This caused initial conflicts, resulting in a self-selection process that reinforced the original founders' culture.

However, as the company scaled from 100 to 1000 employees and beyond, expanding into over 100 countries, maintaining the original culture became impossible. The creative, non-bureaucratic way of doing things had to evolve into a more process-oriented culture. The founders' high standards and relentless drive for excellence led to a culture where employees felt they were never good enough, despite their significant achievements. Recognition was lacking, and people stayed only because of fair compensation. Frustration spread, burnout followed and talent began to leave.

Eventually, the founders had to acknowledge that their success was in jeopardy if they didn't change their approach. With my guidance, they realized they needed to take personal responsibility for how they provided feedback, recognized achievements and celebrated successes. This led to a cultural shift that began to view employees as whole individuals rather than just "task machines."

THE RECOGNITION CHALLENGE FOR LEADERS

While recognition is an important tool in creating a balanced belonging in organizations it cannot come without addressing the fear of many senior leaders – that too much recognition can soften the urge to always become better and strive to achieve more. Many leaders I have worked with believe that spending too much time on 'sugarcoating' prevents people from growing, improving and achieving more. Moreover, they fear losing their authenticity if they are overly concerned with others' feelings at the expense of candid feedback.

My answer to these concerns is that there is no need for sugarcoating. But equally, there's no need to deliver the truth in the faces of their employees in a way that undermines and doesn't acknowledge their efforts and hard work.

I remember a CEO of a software company who consistently provided honest and direct feedback to people presenting ideas to him. Too often, this feedback came across as aggressive, leaving people feeling hurt, demotivated, or even breaking down. When I pointed this out to the CEO, he was open to listening, as the last thing he wanted was to harm his team or undermine their motivation.

I suggested that when an employee presents something that doesn't seem right, he should pause before proving them wrong and try a different approach. Given his background in technology, he asked with a smile if I could give it to him as an 'algorithm.' I laughed and then sent him what he wanted – a formula he could use in these situations:

1. **Ask to Understand**: Start by trying to understand the thinking behind what was presented. Ask about the reasoning, assumptions and the process that led to their conclusions.

2. **Acknowledge Genuinely**: Find something genuinely impressive in their approach, and acknowledge the effort and creativity involved. This should be sincere – no sugarcoating – so they feel recognized for their work.

3. **Challenge Graciously**: Point out any gaps you still see and suggest an alternative direction for follow-up research or action. Give them the opportunity to learn and grow, rather than feel like they have failed.

Many executives face a common dilemma: how to drive excellence while empowering people to be their best. The key is to balance direct feedback with genuine curiosity about the employee's perspective. This involves pausing automatic judgment and moving beyond a "downloading" style of listening, especially during stressful times. By being open-minded, leaders can better recognize the thought process behind an employee's approach and acknowledge their efforts. This does not mean ignoring what's missing; rather, it means framing those gaps in a way that encourages further growth and creativity. Acknowledging someone's work while challenging them constructively can foster a positive environment where both excellence and authenticity thrive.

REASONS FOR DISENGAGEMENT

Another reason people feel lost in organizations is that they can't find themselves in the relentless pursuit of goals and Key Performance Indicators (KPIs). Their values and moral compass may not always align with the organization's approach. This tension becomes more severe when organizations grow and pass a specific tipping point in their size. In large organizations decision-makers must balance seeing employees as both people and 'head counts.' That is a necessity for ensuring profitability and shareholder satisfaction. As the organization becomes increasingly driven by market dynamics, people often feel like small cogs in a large machine, forced to compromise their values. This disconnect ultimately leads to disengagement, as people lose meaning and the sense of identity that makes work fulfilling.

'Dunbar's Number' comes to mind here – research suggests that humans are generally capable of maintaining only 150 meaningful relationships. Malcolm Gladwell wrote about this concept in *The Tipping Point* (Gladwell 2002), using the example of Gore-Tex, where founder Bill Gore ensured that new offices or factories were opened once a location reached 150 people. This structure maintained a feeling of community and cohesion. Most large organizations, however, organize themselves around functional and business needs rather than human connection, which, while efficient, often leads to disengagement and burnout.

In today's organizations, many people feel burned out, often dreaming of retirement or financial independence that would allow them the freedom to choose how to spend their time. To cope with burnout, people often turn to self-care practices like yoga, meditation, vacations, hobbies and other wellness activities. The underlying assumption is that balancing work and personal life can sustain mental and physical health. However, this approach often addresses only the symptoms, not the root causes of burnout.

Burnout in the workplace is not just a personal issue but a systemic one. Employees tend to accept stressful environments as unchangeable, believing it is impossible to negotiate better conditions with their superiors. Many employees I've met in large organizations feel powerless to change these environments and resign themselves to a reality that continues to erode their wellbeing – no matter how many self-care activities they pursue. While these wellness activities can be beneficial, we must also acknowledge the significant impact that the work environment has on mental health.

To understand how organizations contribute to stress and disengagement, it is helpful to consider recent research conducted by Gallup and others. The main factors contributing to burnout and disengagement are:

1. **Sense of unfairness**: Injustice, bias, favoritism and inappropriate behavior from peers or managers can create a sense of inequality. Employees who reported experiencing unfair treatment are 2.3 times more likely to feel 'high burnout' compared to those who feel fairly treated.

2. **Overload and time pressure**: When employees feel overwhelmed by an excessive workload, they often experience a loss of control that leads to stress and burnout. Overloaded workers expect support from their managers, and the absence of this support exacerbates the stress. Furthermore, constant time pressure, fueled by a culture where 'everything is always urgent,' contributes to exhaustion and ultimately reduces productivity.

3. **Lack of managerial support**: Employees facing challenging situations without the backing of their direct managers are more likely to experience frustration, disappointment and eventually burnout.

4. **Ambiguity in job Expectations**: Ambiguity in job roles and responsibilities or a lack of alignment between an employee and their manager can lead to frustration. In creative roles, where outcomes are harder to define, ongoing dialogue is essential – but the skills needed for such conversations are often lacking on both sides.

5. **Micromanagement**: Excessive control from managers conveys distrust, gradually eroding an employee's sense of accountability, reducing creativity, and fostering pleasing behavior rather than courageous innovation.

6. **Lack of career and professional development**: Employees want opportunities to grow, develop and progress. The absence of development opportunities often leads to feelings of being stuck, resulting in frustration or diminished self-esteem.

7. **Failure to Listen to Employees**: A rigidly hierarchical culture that dismisses bottom-up ideas stifles creativity. This means the organization loses valuable insights from its employees and fosters apathy, especially in an era where innovation is critical for success.

8. **Lack of Recognition and Appreciation**: Recognition is crucial for maintaining engagement and fighting burnout. Employees need to feel that their contributions are noticed and valued.

9. **Blurring Work-Life Boundaries**: The shift to remote work and increased expectations for availability have blurred work-life boundaries. Constant connectivity creates an 'always on' mode, draining energy from employees and impacting their personal lives.

10. **Depressing Workspaces**: While hybrid work has become more common, many employees still need to come into the office. However, most office spaces lack inspiration and feel gloomy, unlike the creative environments seen in tech companies like Google or Facebook. The atmosphere of a workspace – its lighting, colors, sounds and even smells – has a significant impact on employees' energy levels, and creating an energizing space doesn't necessarily require large investments, just thoughtful design.

THE COMMON THREAD: THE LOSS OF HUMANITY

These factors lead to a deeper, systemic issue: they strip away the humanity of employees, reducing them to mere resources. The common thread among all these reasons is that they overlook the individual's need to be recognized as a whole person. Whether it's a lack of fairness, absence of support, micromanagement, or blurring boundaries between work and personal life, each of these factors diminishes the worker's autonomy, creativity and inherent value. Employees end up feeling small, undervalued and disconnected, losing the sense of meaning and engagement that makes work fulfilling.

To truly address burnout and disengagement, leaders must recognize and respond to these underlying dynamics. They need to create environments where people are not only productive but also treated as unique individuals with aspirations and needs. The future of work must go beyond efficiency – it must be centered on the right of every individual to feel whole, valued and genuinely included, while retaining their uniqueness and sense of humanity.

THE NEXT GENERATIONS

It is even more urgent as we welcome the young generation to the world of work. Gen-Z is much more aware than previous generations of their own needs and put them ahead of work. They say: "I'd rather be unemployed than unhappy."

When my son entered the workforce recently after finishing high school, he started a job at a computer company. They had a great team but worked for a very tough boss. One day, the boss saw my son picking up a chocolate bar wrapper that someone had left behind and putting it in the trash can. The trash can didn't have a trash bag. The boss shouted at my son aggressively, saying he shouldn't throw garbage into a trash can without a plastic bag. My son was surprised and couldn't accept it. He resigned the same day. I cannot imagine myself doing that 25 years ago. It's a different generation.

My parents worked the same job from the beginning of their careers until retirement. To date, I've changed jobs about six times and switched between being a salaried employee to a self-employed freelancer. I belong to Generation X (born 1965–1980). My generation accounts for about 33% of the workforce in the US and will drop to 10% by 2040. Millennials (Gen Y; born 1981–1996) now make up about 35% of the global workforce and by 2040 they will be 43%. Gen Z (born 1997 onward) comprises currently 11% of the US workforce and is projected to be 35% by 2040.

Millennials are very different from mine and my parents' generation. Twenty-one per cent of them changed jobs in the past year. Six out of every ten millennials wants to change jobs at any point in time. Only 29% are engaged in their place of work. This is the least-committed generation in the workplace compared to previous generations. The data shows that future generations are going to be even less engaged.

Why is that so important? Because we must adapt work to the emerging future. The new generation of workers is less attached to traditional structures, more informed and connected, and more flexible to make career changes and seek meaning and purpose. They ask without apologizing: "What's in it for me?" They won't give up their identity to just be part of an oppressive workplace. They truly wish to belong in a better way. In many ways, they are the model generation for balancing both sides of the Belonging Paradox, refusing to compromise on either.

WHAT IS THE NEEDED CHANGE?

Many organizations understand the need for change and adapt their management strategies to the expectations of Millennials and future generations. However, not all strategies bring the desired results. According to Forbes, before COVID-19, 53% of Millennials reported feeling burnout at work. These figures rose to 59% at the height of the COVID-19 period. Statistics don't lie, and if there are so many employees in organizations who don't feel committed and emotionally connected to the workplace, the necessary change probably hasn't occurred yet.

But what change needs to happen? Which of the many strategies to increase employee engagement should organizations choose and invest in?

The basic psychology of human beings has not changed, despite sociological changes between generations. Therefore, Herzberg's theory of intrinsic (motivators) and extrinsic (hygienic) factors from 1959 is still relevant. According to this theory, there are internal factors that motivate a person to work such as: challenge at work, recognition and appreciation, meaning, accountability, participation in decision-making and a sense of purpose. In the absence of these factors, motivation, and therefore commitment to work, will be low. On the other hand, extrinsic (in Herzberg's language: hygienic) factors are necessary for a person to be satisfied with work, necessary but not sufficient conditions, such as: fair salary, social benefits, working environment conditions, vacations, stability, etc. Today's strategies for increasing employee engagement can be divided according to the factors proposed by Herzberg:

Examples of extrinsic-hygienic strategies:

- **Wellness programs**: Upgraded health insurance, gym memberships, etc.
- **Enhanced benefits packages**: Improved social benefits such as additional vacation days, stock options, etc.
- **Upgraded workspace**: Amenities like pool tables, nap and rest rooms, and free drinks and snacks.
- **Supportive technologies**: Providing cutting-edge tools and equipment to minimize frustration and enhance job performance, such as state-of-the-art laptops and electric cars.

- **Recreational activities**: Organizing fun days, happy hours and company vacations.

Examples of intrinsic strategies (motivations):

- **Enhanced job roles**: Adding interest, challenge and responsibility to roles.
- **Open dialogue**: Fostering an organizational culture of continuous communication and recognition between managers and employees.
- **Career development**: Providing clear paths for career progression and management opportunities.
- **Learning and development**: Encouraging employees to learn new skills and engage in professional development.
- **Promoting values**: Upholding values of equality, diversity, inclusion, and social and environmental responsibility.

In light of all the findings described above, it can be assumed that there is an increase in the importance of intrinsic factors among Millennials and Gen Z, and organizations would do well to invest more resources and creative thinking in developing programs that will increase employee motivation to belong, and strengthen an individual's sense of self-worth and balance of individuality and belonging.

Having explored the complex relationship between individuals and organizations, we now turn our attention to a crucial aspect of this relationship: employee engagement. Engagement goes beyond mere productivity – it's about emotional connection, fulfillment and creating workplaces where people truly feel they belong. In the next chapter, we'll unpack what engagement really means, why it remains a persistent challenge for organizations, and how a deeper focus on uniqueness and belonging can foster an environment where everyone thrives.

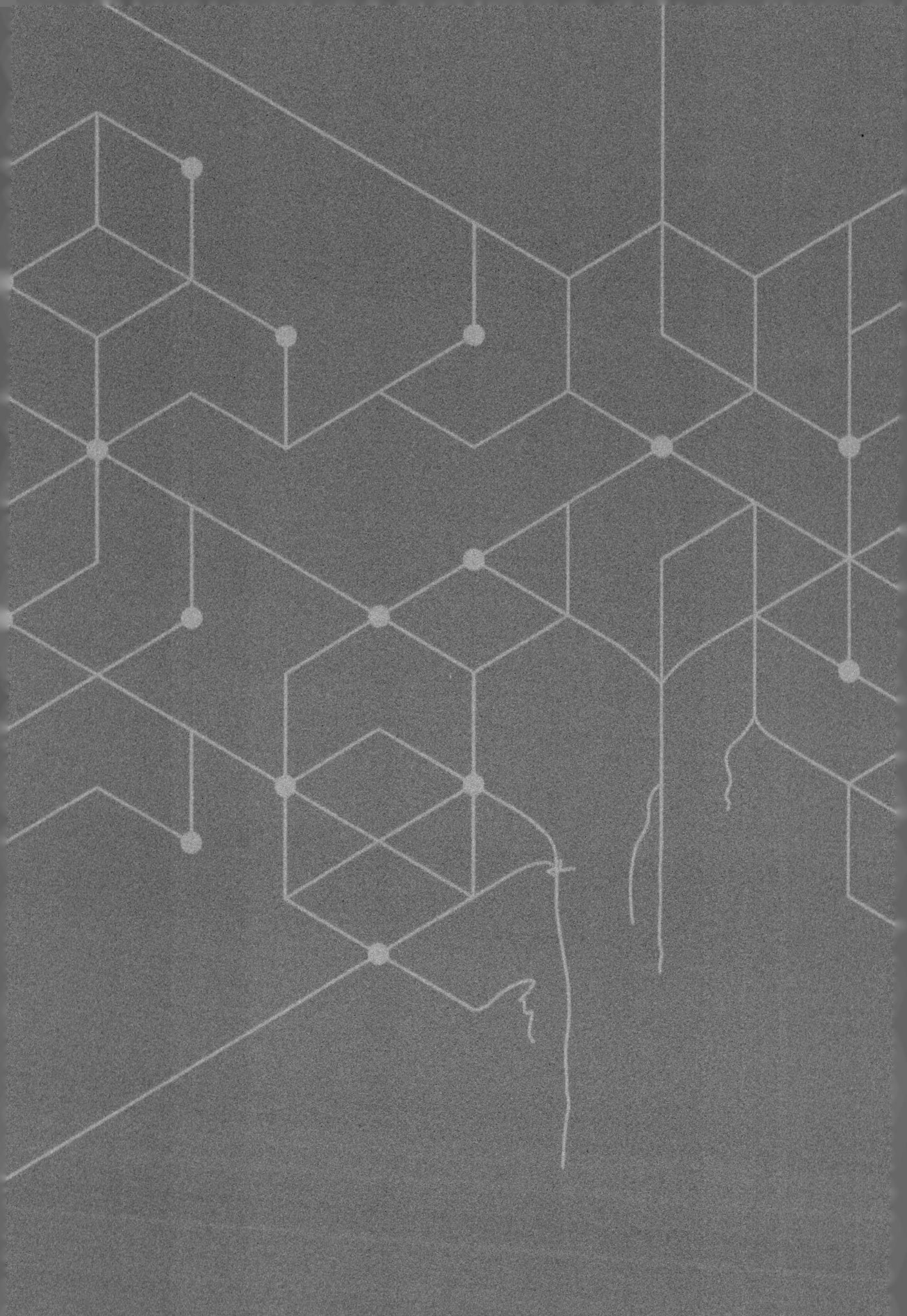

CHAPTER 9

EMPLOYEE ENGAGEMENT

Professional literature in the field of HR identifies engagement and talent retention as the main challenges for organizations today. But what exactly is **engagement**? It is a term that describes a kind of commitment, similar to putting a ring on a fiancée's finger, signifying a promise or a pledge. Are we expecting that employees will have an emotional connection to the organization beyond the formal connection? That's an understandable expectation. Every manager wants their employees to show motivation and willingness to invest in work beyond the minimum required. But this cannot be achieved if employees don't feel fairness, balanced and healthy.

After all, if employees do what they love under conditions that are good for them, their motivation to contribute should flow naturally. Why, then, is engagement needed? Maybe because the job doesn't quite fit the employees' dreams? Maybe because there's a chance that the employee will feel exploited, and then you have to make sure they're committed? Maybe because organizations have become so large and impersonal that HR professionals need tools to identify the weak links and anticipate a decline in commitment?

Perhaps the word engagement is actually a cover for the fact that people don't feel like they belong deeply to organizations. Perhaps the organizations of the 21st century are not designed to provide what people in the 21st century need (and have always needed): personal expression and a sense of healthy belonging. Uniqueness should be a leading principle in restructuring organizations. When this goal is achieved, the need to measure and operate systems to strengthen employee engagement will be redundant. Belonging and personal expression are the most powerful tools an organization can offer its members.

PARADIGM SHIFT: FROM RESOURCES TO PEOPLE

The change required in the workplace is not merely a first-degree change (a change within the boundaries of the existing paradigm) but a second-degree change (a paradigm shift). The dominant paradigm in the world of work, from the days of Frederick Taylor to the present (including Herzberg's theory), is that the organization operates like a machine designed to produce a product efficiently and effectively. Consequently, employees are viewed as resources that should enhance the machine's efficiency, much like raw materials, work processes and management methods are resources. This perspective is evident in the fact that most organizations refer to the department dealing with employees as 'human resources.'

Some organizations have recognized the absurdity of this term and have renamed the department that deals with people to 'People' or similar terms, with leaders titled CPO (Chief People Officer). However, this change is often only cosmetic, and a deeper transformation is necessary to shift the entire organizational perception, placing people at the forefront.

The paradigm shift involves viewing the organization as a place of people, for people, and within a community of people. As such, it must prioritize the wellbeing of its people. The business goals of organizations, while important, cannot take precedence over the people. This means that a leader should never lie, discriminate or humiliate others in any situation, even if it is for a very important business goal. Where there is a conflict between business goals and the welfare and dignity of the people, organizations must find ways to ensure that the wellbeing and dignity of the people who work in and are affected by the organization receive the highest priority.

REIMAGINING THE FUTURE ORGANIZATION: BEYOND TECHNOLOGICAL DISGUISE

When you think about the organizations of the future, you immediately envision robots and artificial intelligence. You think of machines that learn and improve on their own, and mountains of data that enable organizations to provide accurate, focused and efficient service. These services are tailored to specific customer needs, all while bypassing bureaucracy and distance.

However, it is difficult to find descriptions of the organization of the future in terms of its attitude toward people. Is this because, in the age of robots, people will no longer be needed? Or is it because our thinking about organizations hasn't advanced as quickly as technological progress?

While we are already seeing self-driving cars on the road, robots replacing humans in industry, and telemedicine solutions substituting for medical professionals, there is little change in the basic structure of organizations. They remain primarily focused on maximizing shareholder profit above all other stakeholders. The current economic structure perpetuates an obsession with achieving faster, stronger and bigger results – growth at any cost, or the risk of stock prices falling and losing to competition.

Unless there is a fundamental change in this structure, organizations will continue to be unfavorable places for people. This is not because there are bad people in them, quite the opposite. Even great people cannot overcome systemic flaws from within. The system and paradigm must change.

THE ROLE OF ELITES IN LEADING CHANGE

As I write these lines, I am reminded of my time studying for a master's degree at one of the most prestigious schools in the world, Harvard University. From this institution emerged the leaders of the United States through the ages (Obama, George W. Bush, Kissinger, Al Gore, etc.) and business leaders (including Bill Gates and Mark Zuckerberg, who did not complete their studies at the institution). It also has the most Nobel Prize winners of any institution (161).

I attended the Harvard Kennedy School, the School of Public Administration, located in the town of Cambridge near Boston. It was a great, horizon-expanding experience full of power-networking. Some of the classes I took were at the business school, a five-minute walk across the Charles River. This institution, along with several other prestigious institutions in the United States, is the main creator of business and innovation leaders in the country and around the world.

At the same time, it establishes the system that maintains organizations in the old paradigm and fails to bring significant innovation, even when the world is crying out for a new type of organization. One that will be a home and a good place for people, society and the planet.

Since I know from personal experience the quality of this institution, I would expect it to lead the capitalist business world to a safe haven. It should propose and implement new methods of human organization – ones that are good for people, human society, nature and the planet.

One day, 76 years from now, the business class of 2100 will sit in an history of economics class at HBS. The distinguished professor (assisted by an in-ear implanted digital AI whisperer) will tell the students about the organizations that she witnessed at the turn of the millennium. These organizations, she will tell, caused people stress, mental illness, depression, and also polluted, produced unnecessary stuff and convinced people to buy them. The shocked students will find it difficult to believe how such a reality existed and what motivated the people who ran these organizations. They will say to each other with astonishment mixed with a little contempt, "Why did the employees even want to belong to such companies?" Then someone wise will reply, "They had no choice. They felt something was wrong, but they had to provide for their families".

Our organizations, from the industrial revolution till our days, create countless unwanted results on all levels – from personal to global. The feeling is that we live in an era where the unintended consequences of the dominant economic system outweigh the desired results, endangering our common existence on Earth. Something big needs to change. Something that will fundamentally alter the basic order, nature and life as we know it.

Major changes, which fundamentally change the rules of the game, usually happen when an external force shakes the existing system. The extinction of dinosaurs due to a meteorite collision with Earth is an example from nature. The assassination of the Austro-Hungarian crown prince, Archduke Franz Ferdinand, which led to the outbreak of World War I, is a political example. The invention of the wheel, the printing press, the engine, the light bulb, the telephone, and the internet are technological inventions that changed humanity forever.

What is the next shock that will force us to change the paradigm of business and adjust it to the greater good of people, societies and nature? Should it be a catastrophe or can it be a deliberate and organized change, initiated in places like Harvard and other places around the US and the rest of the world? Can we do that without the risk of extinction?

POST-COVID WORLD OF WORK

My personal story from the COVID-19 pandemic is not unique and is surprisingly typical of many people around the world. The thought that almost everywhere in the world people have had similar experiences makes this story universal, connecting and bridging people globally.

Personally, I entered the pandemic at the peak of my activity as CEO of Kav-Mashve, the NGO I headed, spending five full years rich in meaning, belonging and personal expression. Managing an NGO with social goals is a complex task full of responsibility. Regardless of the pandemic, I began to feel signs of burnout and the need to pause, stop and recalculate my course.

When the pandemic hit and the government decided on restrictions and lockdowns, we were forced overnight to change the way we operate. We moved all our activities to the internet and began working from home. The radical change injected adrenaline through me and all the other employees, making me momentarily forget that I wanted to leave. With no previous experience in remote working, we had to invent and develop remote methods of training supporting our beneficiaries (mainly college students). It required round-the-clock work, countless Zoom meetings and a very busy schedule. Without thinking too much about the implications – like most of the world – we switched to working from home. The scope of the organization's activity did not decrease, and our online activities proved effective and helpful to our clients.

Working from home was very different from the usual format of working from the office. The most noticeable change was that the amount of travel and commuting dropped to zero, leaving no need to reserve time between meetings. My schedule could be filled with meetings and activities from morning to evening. There were days when I forgot to drink or eat between meetings, and I would end the day with a headache. My partner, who was defined as an essential worker and hence continued to work from her office as usual, observed, "I think you're working a lot harder than usual." Indeed, the intensity increased along with the output and results. All these created a good sense of meaningful action and success in achieving the organization's goals.

At the same time, there was a dissonance between the good feeling and the news coming from outside. I felt uncomfortable telling people who asked how I was doing that I actually felt really good about the whole crisis. I didn't understand how this pandemic, which caused so much suffering to people who got sick and those who lost their jobs, could still feel like an important, great and formative event in the history of the world in general and the world of work in particular. Mythical thoughts crawled into my usually rational head, suggesting that the plague was sent to us from God/nature/superpowers to make us stop, gather, and observe what we are doing as humanity – a kind of modern Noah's Ark story. Simultaneously, there were also less-optimistic thoughts about how quickly humanity forgets such incidents and represses them as if they never happened. Would the changes that began during the pandemic remain with us even afterward?

One of my favorite questions in the Zoom workshops we gave during this period was: What are the good things that have happened to you since the outburst of the pandemic and the transition to working from home? A sample of the answers included: more time at home and with family, less travel and time spent in traffic, time to think and focus on career changes, more time for sports, reading, watching favorite shows, and more opportunities to get to know neighbors and the local community. Of course, there were also negative aspects, such as too much time in front of screens, the invasion of work into home space, some people not being able to express themselves in the virtual space, and not everyone feeling comfortable opening their cameras – discriminating against those who did.

Remote work, distance learning, remote service delivery, e-commerce, telemedicine and remote mental health care are all processes that existed even before the pandemic. These processes accelerated and made a leap forward by between five and 20 years. What made this leap possible was both necessity and the existence of technological tools for remote work, which organizations were previously hesitant to use. The pandemic left organizations with no choice, and change happened quickly. However, it is not certain that organizational philosophy jumped forward along with the forced change. Will organizations be a better place for people in the post-COVID era? Is the COVID-19 era humanity's opportunity to rebuild the world of work in a way that benefits people and not just as a platform for promoting economic interests? Initial signs show movement in both directions. On the one hand people are much more aware of their ability to choose and not take the organizational demands as granted at the expense of their own mental and physical health. On the other hand, we see more and more organizations pushing people to return to the offices and keep up with the increasing pace and business demands.

I see the pandemic as an opportunity for being more creative and reinvent businesses in a way that will better balance the business and human needs. It is also an opportunity to better balance the basic tension between self-expression and belonging. Hybrid modes of working that enable people to both keep more presence at home and find flexible ways to belong to the company are a blessing. Leaders should not be afraid of letting people find their own ways of being creative and healthy while keeping up with organizational demands. Belonging doesn't always mean coming to the office. It can also mean: I am able to practice my other identities (mother, father, my hobby, my social agenda) while excelling in my work identity. When I feel that the organization allows me to be myself, I am much more ready to bring my best version and add value.

EMPLOYEE-ORGANIZATION RELATIONSHIP IN THE ERA OF POST-COVID-19

The main characteristic of work during and after the COVID-19 era is **remote work**. The importance of the physical location of an organization diminished. There are fewer hours of commuting to the office, fewer traffic jams, less air pollution, fewer flights and fewer casual meetings around the coffee machine. There's also less investment in appearance, what we wear and how we smell, as reality is increasingly shaped by what is seen on electronic screens rather than human encounters.

Under these circumstances, the question arises even more clearly: What is an organization? It's no longer about the physical space, the office design, the hallway interactions or the formal culture in conference rooms. So, what is it then?

It's difficult to say, as we are at the beginning of a new era, but we can guess that the 'organizational glue,' the invisible material that connects the parts of an organization and creates a collective sense of 'our organization,' will have more to do with symbolic meaning. Questions like:

What do we do that is unique? Why do we do this? What is our impact on nature, the world and society? These are questions of meaning. Until now, these questions could be ignored because we met nice people in the office, our coworkers, and together influenced each other to comply and go with the herd. We worked to make a living, to leave home for a place that gave us refuge – each person had their own motivations.

In the age of post-COVID-19, questions of meaning will gain more weight as other components are reduced. It's not that people won't want to work in places where they find meaning. Work is work, and the need to make a living remains the same as it was before the pandemic. However, loyalty to the organization will greatly reduce, and people will become more opportunistic about job offers that come their way. It will be easy to change jobs at the touch of a button for better or more comfortable conditions.

Organizations that do not prepare for this situation and think of new ways to create meaning will suffer from high employee turnover and talent migration, with all the organizational implications that result from this. The temporary imperative requires organizations to think about what will make their employees want to belong, to feel that their organization is a place they are proud of and want to be part of. Personal expression and belonging are more relevant than ever in organizations in the age of post-COVID-19.

The challenge is even greater as personal expression becomes more difficult in the age of remote work. In virtual meetings through the computer, it feels as if the bandwidth of interpersonal communication has decreased. It's like seeing in black-and-white instead of color, hearing in mono instead of stereo. You smell nothing and touch nothing. Interpersonal communication has become a stream of electrons passing from person to person via technology, but it doesn't provide all the possibilities that were there before. Under these conditions, the ability to express oneself, highlight personal abilities and talents, and make a personal mark becomes almost impossible.

Still, people always remain unique and possess different talents. So, we must find ways to allow personal expression in these new conditions. Communication through video screens requires humans to adapt quickly and develop new capabilities, which are already here due to the penetration of smartphones into our lives.

When COVID-19 hit, at Kav-Mashve, the organization I managed, we switched overnight to remote work. We had to quickly adjust to the new situation and support each other during the transition. Our efforts were directed at sensing the challenges and opportunities associated with remote communication, and to better understood what our program participants were going through. This initial effort allowed us to innovate and create solutions that became tools for remote work. For example, we had to learn how to mute and unmute ourselves in the video call. There were funny instances in which people said very important and passionate things, but people could not hear them because they were muted. Since our NGO work was connected to giving minority people a voice we created an idea that used this mute-unmute phenomenon. We decided to create a large conference under the title: "unmute yourself." It was a great event in which people could get training on how to bring their voice in their best version to the virtual-digital space while having to cope with the lockdown.

Not all employees 'slipped into' the new mode easily. Some found it difficult to express themselves in the virtual space. They became quieter and explained in personal one-on-one conversations that it was difficult for them to take up space without eye contact and a sense of physical presence. On the other hand, one employee really flourished. The virtual space brought out a burst of creativity and new initiatives in her. She changed her approach to work and seized the opportunity to express her talent. I noticed this and allowed her to lead several initiatives that advanced the organization during the initial confusion of the pandemic.

Remote work is changing the social map of the organization and creating new 'stars' alongside people who are less adaptive. Since we know that this trend will only intensify, we must develop the skills in all employees to express themselves in virtual spaces and through screens. It is no coincidence that storytelling workshops are flourishing in organizations right now. People understand the importance of telling a story in a captivating and attention-grabbing way, especially when the communication channel is as narrow as a smartphone screen. We need to develop the ability to deliver short messages, stand in front of a screen, conduct meetings remotely, notice group dynamics through the screen and support those who are struggling personally. Employees who fail to express themselves in virtual spaces will become the 'weak links' in the new world of work and will seek other places where they can express their talents. This represents a significant amount of talent that can be lost if this issue is not taken seriously. A sense of belonging and loyalty to an organization is greatly strengthened when people feel they have space for personal expression. The challenge is intensified in the era of remote work.

On the employee side, working from home can be a paradise or a nightmare, depending on how it's implemented. If organizations understand that change is not only physical but deeply psychological and sociological, there is a chance for everyone to benefit. If the organization compensates for physical distance with multiple controls, surveillance and psychological pressure, it will decrease trust between employer and employee, increase burnout, and lead to higher employee turnover.

There is an opportunity here to finally see employees in their full context as human beings rooted in family, community and social contexts, allowing them to realize themselves in all aspects, not only in terms of work efficiency. Staying at home allows employees to be more involved in their home (e.g., childcare, gardening, household chores), in their community (e.g., participation in neighborhood initiatives, involvement in community projects), and in personal development (e.g., extracurricular activities, sports and other hobbies). The hours saved from commuting should be used wisely, allowing employees to focus on their work without neglecting other important areas of their lives.

For example, people who have always dreamed of exercising before work can now do so, gaining more concentration and healthy energy for their workday. Another example is parents who can now help their children get ready for school in the morning, participating in this short but significant activity. Reducing pressure at home can enhance overall wellbeing, benefiting the employee's work performance.

PERSONAL EXPRESSION AS PART OF THE WORK PERSONA

In the past, many employees had to hide or suppress their nonwork-related passions such as creativity and arts, music, sports, animal care, mindfulness, etc. Organizations expected employees to fully dedicate themselves to their work, channeling all their energy toward the success of the organization. Personal interests were often sidelined and, if acknowledged, were limited to happy hours or team-building activities, not as a legitimate part of daily organizational routine.

In the age of COVID-19 and remote work, the integration of the whole self – including all personal interests and identities – has become critical and important. Previously, personal matters were discussed (at best) in one-on-one conversations between employees and their managers or in informal chats among colleagues. Now, remote work provides an opportunity to highlight each employee's uniqueness, including their family, community and cultural background, as part of their full identity within the organization.

When employees feel they can share parts of their personal world (to the extent they are comfortable), there is a greater chance of fostering a sense of belonging. Organizations need to invest in tools that allow employees to express their personal contexts. One such idea is to create video libraries where employees can present parts of themselves that aren't necessarily work-related but contribute to their overall identity.

For example, an organization could build a TED-like video platform where employees give short, engaging talks about their hobbies, unique origin cultures or family traditions. This would increase familiarity among employees and help create an invisible bond that is often missing when physical space becomes less relevant.

Another example is changing the periodical feedback talks between managers and their reports to be a wider opportunity to get to know each other's world and aspirations. The manager can ask the employee questions that are beyond just work-related issues and co-create a plan for the employee's vision and aspirations in life. When managers start to support long-term development visions of their employees, they will gain much deeper engagement, loyalty and a sense of belonging.

These tools, combined with a new policy emphasizing each person's uniqueness in private as well as professional contexts, will strengthen employees' sense of being seen for who they are as unique individuals. This approach will highlight the diversity of the human fabric within the organization and support diversity and inclusion initiatives – topics that had already gained momentum even before the COVID-19 era. In the next chapter, we'll examine how ensuring that everyone feels they belong – without having to hide who they are – can enrich not only individuals but also the organizations they are part of.

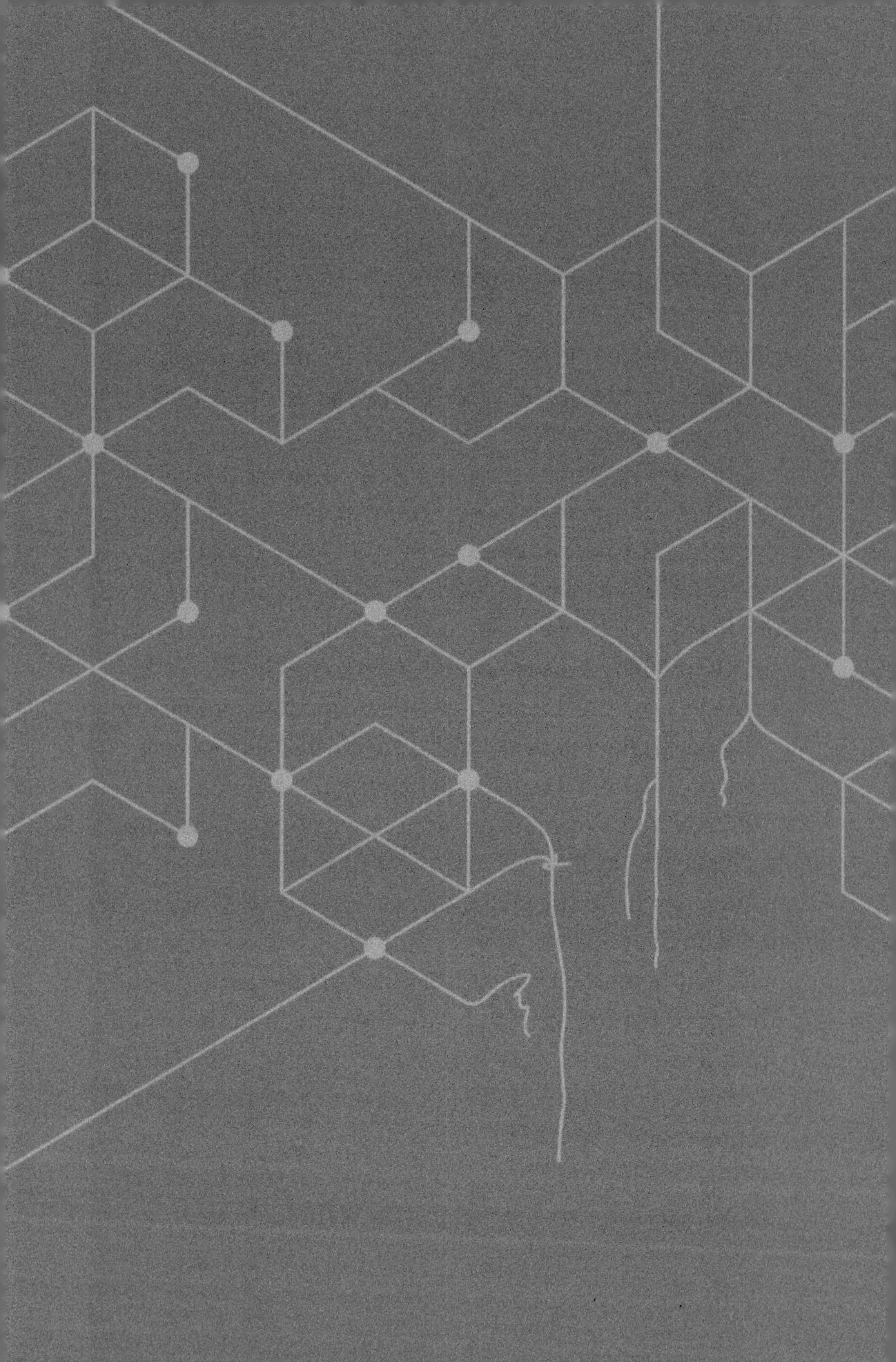

CHAPTER 10

DIVERSITY AND INCLUSION

The way to mastering the Belonging Paradox must go through making sure that everyone has a chance to enter the groups they want to belong to, feel included without needing to cover parts of their identity. This was my main priority in running Kav-Mashve, the NGO that I managed for almost six years. As part of my work at Kav-Mashve, I met with many university students from the Arab society in Israel to discuss their career management. One of the topics we discussed was leadership. I wanted to understand how they perceived this concept, so I asked them a simple question: Think of someone you consider a leader and who they are and what makes them a leader in your eyes. Before I share the answers I received, I ask you, the reader, to think about this question and answer it for yourself before reading further: Who do you consider worthy of being called a leader?

I know that if I were asked this question, I would probably talk about Barack Obama or Martin Luther King, Jr., or even basketball player LeBron James, who, besides excelling in sports, takes political stands without fear. But the answers from the young people from the Arab society in Israel surprised me, and they were very consistent every time I performed this simple exercise: Most students pointed to their fathers or grandfathers. A lesser number pointed to their grandmothers and mothers. The stories were always very moving. For example, a student shared how his father was the hero of his childhood, built a successful business with his own hands and supported the family. Then a financial crisis occurred, and the father went bankrupt and also suffered health setbacks. The child (the storyteller) had to take responsibility at home and help his mother take care of the other siblings. They suffered a few years of hardship in which he had to go to work in parallel to school but they never lost hope that things could become better. The father, who despite his health issues and business situation, always radiated optimism, recovered, and rebuilt the business while showing everyone that 'everything is possible.' This was an example that I heard many times in different versions. The common thread in all of the stories was that the leader was almost always the father or another very close relative and not an external world leader like many of us would choose.

This story opened my eyes. Behind each of these impressive students was a fascinating life story that unfolded in an environment and narrative that, to me, was foreign, unfamiliar, and even unpredictable. Even more so, the language we spoke was different even if the words we used were the same. They understood the concept of 'leadership' and many other concepts entirely differently from how I did. This difference was a hidden one, and only by delving into the conversation could it be discovered. I realized that, despite considering myself a sensitive and attentive person, I could also miss the nuances of the diversity and uniqueness of people.

My work at Kav-Mashve was to connect the young Arab talents and the business workforce in Israel – I had to have conversations with many managers from the business sector about the importance of diversity and inclusion. Although I was focused mainly on the integration of Arab citizens, the discussion about diversity and inclusion was relevant to any ethnic, gender or cultural group that was underrepresented in the workplace. All the managers always expressed very positive attitudes toward the importance of employment diversity ("I am very much in favor"), but the data showed that the connection between positive attitudes and implementation was not simple at all. I heard various reasons why there is no adequate representation of Arab university graduates in commercial companies in the economy, such as: "We advertise job openings but do not receive enough résumés from Arab candidates," "We really want diversity but as a competitive company in a competitive market, we cannot hire people just on the basis of affirmative action – we are looking for the best," etc. Many managers even claimed they advertise job openings in Arabic but still do not receive almost any résumés from Arab candidates. I found a lot of goodwill and awareness of the need for change in the business sector, but very few capabilities and tools to realize this change.

To succeed in the task of organizational diversity and inclusion, several 'gates' must be passed, as will be described further on. This requires organizational preparation and the designation of individuals who will be responsible for the various gates. The data and reality on the ground show that it is not easy to integrate 'different' people into business workplaces – so if the organization really wants this, it must approach the task like any other business task, set goals, build a practical action plan, measure results and reward success.

One organization that managed to help companies make the change and build a practical and meaningful plan for integrating workers from the Arab society is called Co-Impact. This NGO, which was established through a civilian initiative and sponsored by the president of the

State of Israel, managed to gather 50 CEOs of the largest companies in the Israeli economy and enlist their commitment to diversity and inclusion. Co-Impact offered these companies organizational consulting and assistance in building and implementing the action plan. Companies that entered the process managed to significantly increase the recruitment of workers from Arab society. Part of its success was in making this effort an important part of the Corporate Social Responsibility of the companies and to be acknowledged by the president of the state as a national, important effort. However, as described below, recruiting 'different' employees is not enough and, the issue must be viewed in a holistic and systemic way.

To succeed in recruiting candidates from excluded communities and successfully integrating them into organizations, it is first necessary to understand the barriers and deep reasons this does not happen naturally. On the employers' side, the main barriers are lack of familiarity with candidates from excluded groups, lack of understanding of unique cultural characteristics, and lack of recognition of the need to build trust and take proactive steps to encourage candidates to apply. Racism and prejudice were not in the forefront. If it existed, it was well covered.

On the candidates' side, there were different types of barriers: self-confidence and fear of failure, cultural understanding (not just language but the entire cultural context of the majority society), geographical distance from employment centers and lack of social-community support. For example: a man who wanted to study theater was not supported because it was not a common occupation in this society, or a woman who wanted to work far from the family home was held back for traditional reasons. All these factors led to an avoidant behavior in which only about 50% of Arab graduates in Israel were applying for jobs that required academic training in the Israeli business sector. How can people from a minority group even start to feel that they belong if they don't try to apply and stay isolated?

At Kav-Mashve, we mainly addressed the psychological aspect of self-confidence and empowerment of the students and encouraged them to believe in their right to succeed. However, working with candidates alone was not enough. An organization that wanted to successfully integrate candidates from excluded communities had to do more than just wait for the marginalized candidates to send their résumés. As mentioned before, they had to pass through several 'gates':

THE FIRST GATE – OUTREACH AND BE PROACTIVE

Identify candidates for recruitment at the earliest possible stages, even before they complete their academic and professional training. Early involvement of employers in training processes will create several positive effects: 1) Familiarity of the organization with the candidates and creating a relationship with them from early stages; 2) Familiarity of the candidates with the employers and creating trust and confidence that are so crucial; 3) The ability of employers to influence the training curriculum (in collaboration with training institutions) so that candidates acquire the tools and skills needed to succeed quickly in the job market upon graduation.

THE SECOND GATE – IDENTIFY THE GEM

Usually, the interviewer comes from the dominant part of society with a different cultural background than the interviewee. The challenge is to recognize the talent and potential of the candidate despite differences in accent, language, culture, etc. Many interviewers let these differences distract them instead of focusing on the relevant qualities and skills for the job. Ultimately, the recruiting managers are team leaders who need to meet goals and show results in the short term. The battle for talent is a big issue for any organization, and by being open to diverse talents, the organization can benefit greatly and achieve its business goals more effectively.

THE THIRD GATE – ONBOARDING

The first days, weeks and months of the new diverse employee are the hardest and require special effort. Often, the new recruit was accepted into a team where they are the only 'different' ones. This is inherently difficult because they have no one to share the challenges and uncertainties with. The initial period is when the odd feeling of being different is at its peak, even though many organizations make great efforts to ease new employees' integration and be welcoming. It is not always easy to see the difficulty that a new diverse employee goes through. The new employee usually tries to show that everything is cool, everything is under control and keeps the difficulties inside to avoid showing weakness. Not only do they feel they need to prove themselves exceptionally, but they also cannot receive support from their colleagues who do not always know what they are going through. Part of the pressure and the need to learn and adapt quickly causes the employee to adapt quickly, change their behavior, language and culture to the standard used in the organization. When succeeding in doing so they start to feel 'one of us.' This is very gratifying in the short term, but the danger is that in the longer term, the employee will not express their diversity, will not feel free to be authentic, and will hide parts of themselves from their colleagues and the organization. This results in a double loss. The organization does not benefit from the added value of diversity: a different style of thinking, a new way of acting and the ability to solve problems by combining different styles. Additionally, the employee will not really feel at home and will not develop the deep connection that will keep them in the organization for a long time. Onboarding should be a two-fold effort. The first is to help the new employee to adapt fast. The second is to be curious and welcoming to the different flavors and colors of the new employee and make them legitimate and socially wanted.

THE FOURTH GATE – INTEGRATION AND INCLUSION

The new employee is absorbed and already feels part of the team or community. However, the inclusion paradox is that the success of their integration often stems from assimilation and hiding unique and different characteristics, from trying to be like everyone else. The term 'covering' used for this phenomenon was coined in 1963 by sociologist Erving Goffman and was further explored by legal scholar Kenji Yoshino in his book *Covering* (Yoshino 2006). A Deloitte study among 1269 employees in 20 large companies in the US found that 60% of employees had to hide parts of themselves to fit into mainstream culture, and 66% of those who reported hiding parts of themselves said the phenomenon significantly harmed their self-image at work (Deloitte 2023). Instead of the new employee being part of the organization because they are authentic and true to their original and unique identity, they actually assimilate into the dominant culture. The problem is that they will almost always feel like a 'tail to the lions,' inferior, because the rules of the mainstream culture are not always clear and easy for them to apply.

Many organizations make efforts to ensure that employees from minority groups are not left behind and that they are equal partners. However, it is very challenging to shake off the idea that 'equality does not necessarily mean similarity.' Each employee should be given the conditions to thrive by being their true self, rather than by conforming to a one-size-fits-all standard. This requires managers to put in significant effort to understand each employee, recognize their strengths and limitations, understand their language and culture and allow them to express themselves authentically. This can sometimes conflict with the need to create a uniform standard within the team – this is precisely the art required of a manager.

As a result of the covering phenomenon described above, many employees do not realize their potential, which manifests in a lack of advancement up the ranks: many do not move up the ladder and do not reach team leadership or senior management positions. One of the most striking statistics that I learned while working in Kav-Mashve was that only 0.3% of managers in the business sector are from the Arab community (which makes up 21% of the Israeli population). Inclusion of employees in an organization cannot stop at the entry levels and production floors. An organization that aims for true inclusion must consider that diverse employees are entitled to maintain their uniqueness, and this is important and beneficial both to the individual and the organization. There is no reason why diverse employees shouldn't be promoted to senior positions in organizations just like any others from the majority community.

At Kav-Mashve, we understood the importance of promoting employees from the Arab community and launched several prestigious management development programs in collaboration with the Executive Education courses at Tel Aviv University business school. We were able to reach a rate of 80% promotion to those who participated in our programs. A promotion of an employee from a marginalized group to a managerial position has several impacts: 1) The promoted manager serves as a role model for young people from their original community; 2) They prove and accustom the organization to the fact that anyone from any group and background can be a manager; 3) Managers from excluded groups bring more sensitivity to diversity and inclusion processes and help to facilitate a deep change in the organization.

THE FIFTH GATE – MASTERING THE BELONGING PARADOX

Organizations today face a general problem of a declining sense of belonging. Employees stay, on average, no more than three years in an organization, whereas in our parents' generation, people worked their entire lives in organizations until retirement. A recent Gallup poll from 2024 found that only 30% of employees in US companies feel engaged at their workplace. This is a tough starting point if we want people to feel they belong and feel at home in their workplace. The belonging challenge is even harder when we consider the high rate of 'workplace covering' data reported earlier. When people are busy covering, they do not feel comfortable or at home. Therefore, the challenge for organizations interested in promoting diversity and inclusion is the challenge of mastering the Belonging Paradox. Deloitte understood this principle. In their 2021 DEI (diversity, equity and inclusion) report within Deloitte, they emphasized the importance of coupling inclusion and belonging and defined the organizational goal in this area as follows: "Strengthening our inclusive culture to empower people to be their authentic selves, feel like they belong, have courageous conversations respectfully and develop genuine relationships."

Deloitte states that it is important to them that employees bring their authentic selves to work without the need for covering. They understand that this will lead to a stronger sense of belonging, and they even suggest how to achieve this through courageous conversations (courageous in that sense is conversations about sensitive topics that are not necessarily in consensus), leading to the formation of real and deep relationships.

Deloitte likely understands the importance of balancing the Belonging Paradox. This has a direct impact on the employees feeling that they are in the right place for them, which will make them more likely to stay longer in the organization and be more effective and creative. Beyond the individual aspect, it is clear that a group of employees who feel at home creates more cohesive and effective teams and an organizational culture that is more pleasant to be a part of and in which to create.

Mastering the Belonging Paradox is now the next step for most organizations focused on diversity and inclusion. It is no longer just about ensuring the diversity and inclusion of people from minority or excluded groups. It is about being sensitive to and valuing every individual as they are. It is about managing 'otherness,' which is rooted in all of us as unique human beings.

DIVERSITY AND TEAM DYNAMICS

Most readers are likely familiar with the experience of being part of a team – whether at work, through volunteering, in the community, or any other setting where people come together to achieve a common goal. Being part of a great team can be energizing and inspiring, while being part of a less-effective team can lead to feelings of isolation, sadness and a loss of self-confidence. Throughout my career, I have experienced both.

One of the least-successful teams I experienced was when I was invited to join a group of NGO leaders to form a collective impact force on a specific social topic. Everyone was very polite and friendly at the beginning. The problem arose when it became clear that not everyone shared the same goal, and hidden interests overshadowed the stated goal. Distrust developed, and a gap emerged between the spoken language in the meetings and the intentions behind the scenes. I felt that when I tried to be authentic and express my concerns, I got a push back and felt the undercurrents against me. My participation in this team gradually turned from an important task into an emotional burden. After a while of trying to change the feeling and offering suggestions for change, I gave up and decided to leave. Looking back, the experience was difficult because I couldn't feel a sense of belonging, despite the importance of the common goal. The feeling of not belonging left me isolated and sad and eventually made me realize that it was better to leave. I learned that sometimes, despite the desire not to give up on oneself, it is good to leave and distance oneself from an environment that does not allow you to feel your best.

Fortunately, there were also many good team experiences. One of them was when I participated in a professional team that wrote a professional article on the role of organizational development consultants. I was the youngest member of the team. There were about five or six seasoned consultants and researchers, each bringing a lot of perspective and experience. The team meetings were fascinating. I learned a lot from the experienced members, but I also felt I could bring my unique voice and that the other members listened and incorporated it into the joint product. The fact that we had different backgrounds, ages and thinking styles did not interfere with the process but rather contributed greatly to the richness of the discussion and the effectiveness of turning theoretical ideas into practical principles. The emerging joint article was a source of pride. I felt I was learning and contributing equally, and I was left with a positive experience that remained with me for years to come.

KEY FACTORS IN TEAM SUCCESS: BELONGING AND UNIQUE CONTRIBUTIONS

In both stories from my personal history, the main factor that distinguished the successful team experience from the less successful one was my sense of belonging – how much the team members saw and appreciated me for who I was, without expecting me to become someone else. Additionally, in the successful team, I valued what I gained from being part of that team: learning from different people with different styles and the feeling that a new creation was being formed from each one's unique contribution. In other words, the successful team had a good balance between the belonging and the unique voice.

Teams are the cornerstone of building organizations. Therefore, giants like Google invest significant resources to understand what makes a great team. In the 'Aristotle' project, Google researched the characteristics of excellent teams (Duhigg 2016). Here are the five characteristics they found:

1. **Psychological safety** – Team members feel safe to take risks and be vulnerable in front of each other.

2. **Dependability** – Team members trust each other and fulfill their commitments to meet team and organizational goals.

3. **Structure and clarity** – Team members have clarity about their roles, plans and goals.

4. **Meaning** – The work is personally important to each team member.

5. **Impact** – Team members feel that their work matters and creates significant change.

'Psychological safety' is, no coincidence, the first and most important component identified by Google regarding excellent teams. It aligns with everything described above: the ability of a person to feel good about who they are and receive support from their team members even when taking risks or making mistakes. The confidence to be oneself – without embarrassment, without apology and with pride – is the key to self-actualization within a team. Teams that foster an environment where individuals can truly actualize themselves are the most successful.

However, psychological safety alone is not enough for team success. Dependability is crucial and is deeply connected to the level of trust among team members. Without trust, psychological safety is compromised, and vice versa. Trust is built through listening, acceptance and the assurance that one can rely on the other. It is through trust that the invisible bonds between members, which form a successful team, are created. Trust is established through shared experiences and the confidence that there will be no negative surprises. Therefore, you often hear people in teams ask for transparency. Without it, it is hard to trust. A team with a high level of trust allows everyone to be authentic without the need for pretenses.

The next component identified by Google, structure and clarity, also contributes to creating the overall puzzle of psychological safety. People need to know what is expected of them on both a personal and team level. When things are clear, it creates rules of the game or field boundaries within which one can thrive. However, what happens when job definitions and boundaries become blurred? These situations are very common in today's unpredictable work environment. Yet, some teams thrive more than others even under conditions of ambiguity and rapid change.

The other components found in Google's Aristotle project that are important for team success are directly related to the need for personal expression and meaning for each team member. **Meaning** and **impact** allow each individual to find their unique connection to their work. When people personally identify with the purpose of work and feel they make a difference, that strengthens their sense of wanting to be part of this team, hence belonging.

STRENGTHENING THE BELONGING IN TIMES OF TURMOIL

When I managed Kav-Mashve, the COVID Pandemic caught us by surprise, like all other organizations worldwide. The imposed lockdown and the need to work from home required quick adaptation and changes in management and operation patterns. I remember that the government decided on the first lockdown on Saturday, 14 March 2020, and we had to prepare overnight for continued remote operation. The first decision I made was that we would meet every morning for a team call in addition to our routine weekly staff meeting. This turned out to be a very important decision because the situation was new and unfamiliar to everyone, and we needed to rely on each other to learn and support one another. Working with Zoom technology caused different employees to respond differently. Some employees enjoyed the medium very much and managed to bring out creativity and initiatives that were not there before. Some employees weakened, and their energy levels dropped, and it was clear that the digital medium, along with remote work, was not good for them. One employee stood out above all in her creativity and ability to initiate digital activities that innovated and made a significant impact. This was an employee whose talent I had seen less before the COVID times, and it was precisely the transition to remote work that served her talent well. I encouraged her and pointed out her contribution to everyone. At the same time, I had personal conversations with each of the employees who connected less to the medium, encouraged them, and helped find ways to strengthen them. Agile adaptation to the new situation led to great team success and excellent results. The key was listening to each employee's needs and the ability to allow employees to move, be flexible, find new solutions, but also show sensitivity to those less connected and help them regain their strength in the new situation. But beyond flexibility and adaptation, I learned how important it is to observe and learn more about employees, especially during times of change and uncertainty. The new learning about the employees allowed for a reorganization of roles and responsibilities in the team and, as a result, better personal and team productivity – and a more connected feeling among employees precisely when everything around was in turmoil.

We have discussed the importance of diversity and inclusion that can lead to real belonging without needing to cover our authentic selves. But since we are all different, even if we look alike or come from similar backgrounds, we need to think of the matter from a broader perspective: understanding and managing basic otherness. In the next chapter, we will explore how we can build organizations that excel in managing otherness. We will look at examples of organizations that made that principle the core of their culture.

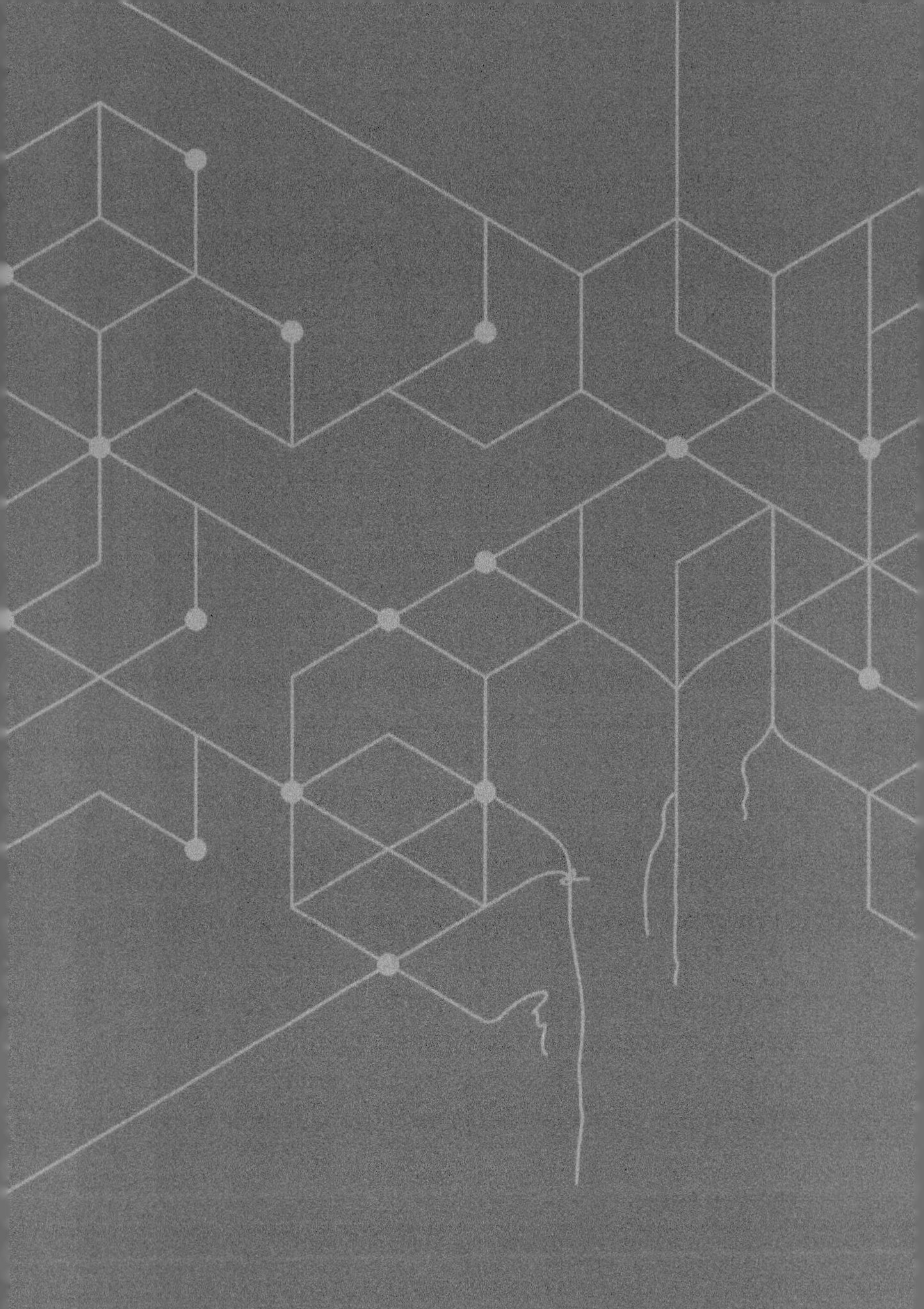

CHAPTER 11

UNDERSTANDING AND MANAGING OTHERNESS

Everyone is born different, making each person unique. While we share many similarities as human beings, we also possess a multitude of differences. I grew up in Israel, surrounded by people similar to me, and was less aware of the diverse cultures and backgrounds of people worldwide, aside from what I saw on my black-and-white TV. Whenever I met people from abroad, I was fascinated by them and tried to stay close to absorb some of the 'otherness' they brought with them.

I remember a story I heard from Daniel H. Kim, an expert in organizational learning from MIT, about the moment he and his family landed in the United States when they emmigrated from Taiwan. Kim was a child then, and when he got off the plane and looked around, all the white people seemed very similar to him. "My first impression was that all these white people looked alike, and I couldn't tell them apart." This is the naïve perspective of a child coming from a distant place and being exposed for the first time to people he had never seen before. I could relate to the story from the opposite direction.

The human brain tends to see differences and variations only in what is familiar to us and part of the landscape we are used to. In contrast, we struggle to see the nuances in things that are new and very different from us. The brain puts it all in one box and creates a designated profile. Cognitive profiling can become dangerous when individuals in positions of power make decisions based on these stereotypical profiles. This can lead to biased and unjust outcomes, as decisions are influenced by oversimplified and inaccurate generalizations rather than a comprehensive understanding of individual differences.

NAVIGATING NEW TEAM DYNAMICS

The same happens when we join a new team with people we didn't know before. Initially, we are so busy understanding the expectations placed on us that it is difficult to deeply notice and get to know those around us. As a result, we primarily remember them by external characteristics and categorization tags. Gradually, however, we start to get to know our colleagues and notice nuances beyond the initial categorizations. As we become more acquainted, we begin to recognize more subtle characteristics, such as personality, habits, temperament, emotional intelligence and more. It then becomes clear that we are different – we think differently, react differently and are sensitive to different things.

BUILDING SUCCESSFUL TEAMS THROUGH DIVERSITY MANAGEMENT

Diversity is everywhere, and no group of people is exactly the same. Understanding this is crucial to building successful teams. We must manage diversity well, and the foundation for this is the ability to see and accept each person as they are. This involves allowing everyone to bring their true selves to every team meeting and shared space without shame or concealment. Achieving this requires a high level of listening, a willingness to compromise, trust, and faith in the goodness of people, even when diversity seems to threaten the fabric of the team.

Creating an inclusive environment within a team necessitates intentional strategies and actions from both leaders and team members. One effective approach is to prioritize active listening and open communication, ensuring that everyone feels heard and valued. Leaders can encourage inclusivity by organizing regular team meetings where each member has the opportunity to share their perspectives and ideas. Implementing diversity-training programs can help team members recognize and address unconscious biases, fostering a more respectful and understanding atmosphere. Research has shown that diverse teams tend to be more innovative and effective, as they bring a variety of viewpoints and problem-solving approaches to the table. Companies like Google and IBM have demonstrated the benefits of embracing diversity and inclusion, with diverse teams driving higher levels of creativity and performance.

HOW TO MANAGE OTHERNESS

Otherness contains additional seeds that are very necessary for organizations today, such as creativity, out-of-the-box thinking, mental flexibility, and more. Managing otherness means building togetherness composed of a variety of different people and creating shared meaning based on acquaintance, curiosity and acceptance. The key to managing otherness in a way that allows everyone to bring themselves fully while simultaneously belonging to the group is the existence of a safe space. Safety is essential so that people are not afraid to express their otherness. When there is legitimacy to be different, unique and other, the result is a multitude of ideas, ways of thinking and creative solutions. Since we are all truly different, there is no need to do much except agree to accept diversity and provide it with a safe space.

Many organizations face increasing competition, and the need to generate creative solutions is existential. The greatest enemies of creativity are cynicism, criticism and the illegitimacy to make mistakes. All of these fall under the definition of an 'unsafe space,' so to create a safe space, we must combat these phenomena and try to shape a culture of encouragement, acceptance, curiosity, legitimacy to err, love of the different and the other. Creating a safe space is very challenging, and few are the spaces where people can be themselves without covering, hiding or living in fear.

THE BROADER CONTEXT OF DIVERSITY, EQUITY AND INCLUSION

From this perspective, dealing with diversity, equity and inclusion (DEI) is just a specific case of managing the general diversity between humans, also known as 'otherness Management.' By actively promoting inclusivity, organizations can create a supportive environment where all team members can thrive, enhancing both individual and collective success.

AN ORGANIZATION BASED ON DIVERSITY AND A SAFE SPACE

Imagine an organization that is founded from the outset on the basis of diversity and a safe space for creativity. It's an unusual thought because most known organizations are established based on a business idea, a product, a service, a market need, etc. But let's assume an organization was created on the basis of human diversity, without any clear tangible goal beyond the desire for shared co-creation that adds value to the world. Suppose those who initially joined the organization were people interested in creating something new and meaningful but did not come 'locked' on a specific idea or thought. And let's assume that all the joiners committed to four principles:

1. To explore diversity.

2. To establish real and authentic relationships that respect diversity.

3. To establish diversity as a central component of the project's DNA.

4. To bring forth from the encounter and friction between the different individuals a common idea that benefits the world.

If such an organization existed, and if it found a beneficial idea that adds value to the world and to the organization's members, it would likely be the ultimate organization for people to belong to: an organization that would not need a diversity officer. Such an organization would enjoy all the advantages of diversity, such as creativity, the ability to access a variety of audiences, high commitment and identification with the organization – and above all – a unique sense of belonging for each of the organization's members.

Today, such for-profit organizations do not exist. Most of the existing organizations try to work on diversity as a way to correct distortions and close gaps that were created over the years when diversity wasn't in their focus or awareness. It starts when the organization is just a newborn start-up. Most startups begin with a group of friends who share common past experiences and already have a solid social fabric. As this group of friends grows the start-up they reach a point in which they need to hire new people. Naturally, they tend to add talents that resemble them, so the beginning of the company is pretty homogenous in terms of people and diversity. The organization's DNA is set by the founders – thereby, the organizational culture becomes homogeneous from the foundation stage, which makes it difficult to add diverse talent later on. However, the reality is that all organizations are actually based on diversity, because people are different, even if they look similar or come from a similar cultural background. I have worked with many startup founders who didn't get along with each other because they had very different management styles and perspectives and they didn't find a good way to communicate and solve their problems. A start-up company is like a baby and the founders are like parents. If they don't work on their relationships and only focus on raising the baby – they will fail to keep the needed bond that is crucial for the baby's development.

If, on the other hand they are good listeners, empathic, do well with conflicts and develop an open and compassionate communication, the chances of success grow massively. These relationships between the parenting founders of startups are the foundation for a DNA of openness, diversity and healthy belonging.

I was always looking to belong in the world of work but also found it challenging for someone like me who always needs to be creative and practice my freedom. At a certain moment in my career, after being part of a few large organizations, I felt like I wanted to create my own organization that would be a great place for people, would celebrate diversity and would support people's creativity. This is when I stumbled upon The-Hub that later became the global Impact Hub Network. In the following paragraphs, I will share the story of establishing The-Hub as a dream workplace and what we can learn from this model for the future of work.

ESTABLISHING THE-HUB IN TEL AVIV

DISCOVERING THE CONCEPT

In 2008, I was introduced to an organization that captured my imagination. It was a physical space, a shared workspace, where people from various countries and backgrounds worked side-by-side, advancing projects aimed at solving social and environmental issues. It was called The-Hub. From the moment I heard about the place in London, I knew

I wanted to visit it. I told my good friend Eli about it, and he immediately got excited about the idea and shared it with two more friends, Yud and Assaf. We were all young, in our 30s, in the midst of building our careers, each in his field. But we knew we didn't want our work, where we would spend most of our adult lives, to be what it was for our parents: a necessity, a compromise and a commitment to institutions we didn't always identify with. We knew we wanted a sense of community at work, of friendship, of interest, curiosity and creativity, alongside a sense of impact and influence on society. Each of us tried to find his way alone and after work hours, we would get together over a beer, complain, weave dreams and enjoy each other's company. We wanted a place that would combine 'work and after work.' So, when I told them about The-Hub, we immediately decided to buy tickets and fly to London to see this promising place.

THE TRIP TO LONDON

Within a few days, we flew to London for a journey that changed our lives in so many ways. The day after our arrival, we left the hotel on our way to The-Hub. We took the underground to Angel Station and walked to the meeting place with our contact person, Leslie. It was a somewhat run-down neighborhood, with old London buildings made of red brick, some housing light industry and some residential, next to a meat and vegetable market. We were excited and felt curious as Leslie led us to The-Hub. We reached the building and walked up three flights of stairs until we reached the door. The moment we walked in, we saw a completely different picture from the gloominess of the neighborhood below. A large, bright hall with high ceilings, green plants everywhere, and people. People working in small teams, each with a small logo describing their project. There was a pleasant buzz of creativity and purpose in the air. Just as it doesn't take me more than five minutes to know if I want to live in an apartment, it didn't take me (and us) more than five minutes to know that this was exactly what we were looking for. A place based on creation, social entrepreneurship, diversity and community. It was a moment that Theory U calls 'Presencing,' a moment when the future reveals itself to you, and you know that your life has changed, and you are ready to do whatever it takes to support this change.

DECIDING TO IMPORT THE CONCEPT TO ISRAEL

After about a half hour of visiting the place, we felt the need to go downstairs and sit in a nearby café to sort out our thoughts and feelings. Over coffee, we realized we wanted to bring this idea home to Israel and open The-Hub in Tel Aviv. We finalized the details with The-Hub's founders and returned home to fulfill the dream.

Back home, we started planning all aspects of the venture, from economic feasibility, defining the customers, services, location and physical structure, to building the community and marketing the idea. To do this, we would meet once a week at a café at a set time and place to create a continuity of planning that would lead to a quick setup. The café was our meeting place where we invited all potential partners, consulted with experts, studied and researched economic models and formulated our shared vision. Ostensibly, we were engaged in planning, but in reality, it was the period when we formed as a team and built the friendship that formed the basis for establishing The-Hub TLV. We understood the weakness arising from our lack of diversity, four middle-class white men, and therefore made sure to meet with potential partners from all parts of Israeli society and build as diverse a community of supporters and partners as possible.

FINDING A PHYSICAL SPACE

Everything was progressing well, and the time came to find a physical space that would fit the vision. The places we checked required extensive renovations and were too expensive for us. Every day I would go through real estate ads for rentals, and one day I found a place that looked suitable. I scheduled a meeting with the landlord and invited my team members to see the place. It was an office of about 200 square meters (exactly the size we were looking for) on the roof of an office building in the center of Tel Aviv. The place captured our hearts. The spacious roof adjacent to the offices was a surprise we couldn't resist. The five-minute principle for identifying desirable real estate worked here too. I knew it was time to close the deal.

MOMENT OF TRUTH

I asked my friends to authorize me to sign a lease with the landlord. It was a critical moment. All the plans and dreams converged at this moment. But to my disappointment, not everyone was ready to take on the financial commitment required to close the lease. Each team member had their own justified reasons, but no one joined me in taking the step at that moment. I thought it was the end of the dream we had woven together because it felt like a real opportunity to move forward and the others were not ready to move. The day ended with a heavy feeling, and I knew that if we didn't take this place, I wouldn't continue with the venture. In the morning, after a sleepless night, I woke up determined to close the deal and take the place, even if it meant doing it without the rest of the team. I called my friends, told them about my intention, and realized they wouldn't join me. That day I signed the lease and took the place to realize the dream of The-Hub.

CONFLICT AND RESOLUTION

It was a moment of conflict between the individual and the group. On the one hand, we had woven the dream of The-Hub as a group, and each team member contributed their skills and talents to the idea. On the other hand, to turn a shared dream into reality, you must take the plunge and decide that at some point you move from planning to execution. After a year of planning, I felt that if my team members didn't move with me to the execution phase, I had to do it myself, even if it meant breaking up the existing team and trying to build a new one. To this day, 15 years later, that moment still hurts me. However, in the tension described in this book between self-expression and belonging to a group, there are no clear-cut answers and no easy solutions when the conflict arises. In this case, my gut feeling was that it was crucial to act immediately, even if this action contradicted the togetherness we had created in the past year. Later, the individual effort turned back into a group effort, albeit in a more limited version. I felt that it wasn't possible to do this alone and called Eli, who had been my closest friend even before this team was formed and offered him the opportunity to join as a full partner without any financial investment on his part. Eli agreed and became a founding partner in establishing the place we had dreamed of.

SETTING OUT

On 1 January 2009, we moved into the new home of The-Hub TLV. The place was empty of people and furniture, and we knew we had to move quickly to implement the plans we had built. We hired an interior designer, invited friends to help build the furniture, and turned the creation process into an ongoing community festival that created the atmosphere we wanted. Within a few days, the place was ready to host the first members of The-Hub, but they were slow to arrive. It turned out that despite the interest expressed by the community members we had built during the planning year, many people did not fully understand the innovative concept of a shared workspace and were not ready to pay monthly membership fees for the right to have a desk and internet, something they could get for free at home or in the cafés of Tel Aviv. We waited patiently and utilized all the social networks and media available to us. Slowly, interested people began to arrive and the first members joined. thank you Yoav, Nitzana, Shelly, Meni, Yarden, Uri, and other dear friends who dared and were early adopters in the days before the world knew about concepts like WeWork and the like. And we began to see the dream take shape.

CREATING A COMMUNITY

We established an organization with one goal: to be a home for people, entrepreneurs, freelancers and free spirits, and to help them realize their dreams through collaboration and community. The place was designed to feel like home to all its members, with minimal rules and bureaucracy, but with high sensitivity to each other's needs. Eli and I played the role of hosts, ensuring everyone was comfortable and taking an interest in them and their work in a gentle manner, according to how much they wanted to share. Our background as management consultants and groups facilitators helped greatly and allowed the members of The-Hub to develop their ventures with the help and connections we could offer. Over time, we offered additional services to the members to strengthen the community, such as 'the whirlpool' – a weekly meeting for entrepreneurs to share, support and brainstorm on entrepreneurial challenges; Hub-Pub, a community gathering with guests for learning and inspiration; shared lunches; parties; and joint events.

AN INNOVATIVE ORGANIZATION

The-Hub TLV was my way of creating an organization that I had not seen throughout my years as an organizational consultant. It was an organization without hierarchy, based on people and relationships between people, engaged in social entrepreneurship and finding solutions for integrating business with closing social and environmental gaps. The core values of this organization were friendship and meaning, which formed the basis for everything else.

The emphasis on community and the relationships within it reflected the importance we placed on the principle of a 'safe space' as a foundation for creativity. At its peak, The-Hub housed a magnificent diversity and variety and was a place where different people could meet, exchange views, get to know each other deeply and create together. The daily innovations at The-Hub stemmed from the encounters between different people and the emphasis we, as hosts, placed on expressing diversity and the freedom to be unique and special.

THE GUIDING PRINCIPLE OF THE-HUB

Anyone can be an entrepreneur: this was our motto at The-Hub. We came to this conclusion from our encounters with people and from the close support we were able to provide to those who were willing to try to be entrepreneurs. We met thousands of people, at The-Hub and outside of it, who felt unfulfilled and unhappy with their routine lives: employees bored with their jobs, people between jobs looking for 'the next thing,' freelancers stuck in a profession they didn't really want. Some had a dream they didn't know how to realize. Others knew they were unhappy with the current situation, and their dream was not clear – just a desire for something they would love and connect with passionately. At The-Hub, we developed a framework that suited everyone. It included three parts: talent, passion and a real problem that needed to be solved.

THE ENTREPRENEURIAL FRAMEWORK

TALENT

Each of these people had a talent, a unique gift they were born with, which they had not always given enough attention to. Many of them neglected their real talents when going to their 'work'. At The-Hub, we tried to guide people to take their talent more seriously and do something with it.

PASSION AND PERSONAL CONNECTION

Different people connect to different issues based on their sensitivities. For example, some people connect more to climate issues, while others connect more to social issues; some were upset by animal abuse, while others were very sensitive to violence against children. Most people would express opinions against violence and injustice – but very few issues will caused people to take action, fight, and embark on a journey, taking them out of their comfort zone. These were exactly the issues people should engage in if they wanted to be entrepreneurs.

A REAL PROBLEM THAT MUST BE SOLVED

There are many problems in the world that need to be addressed, and many needs that must be met, all of which create challenges crying out for solutions. Solutions to these challenges can usually find funding. Funding is like oxygen for the aspiring entrepreneur. In the beginning they have to fund themselves but if they are on the right track, funding may be found later through more institutionalized sources. There are different types of funding: business, philanthropic and governmental. All of them are focused at finding solutions to burning issues and look for passionate and creative entrepreneurs to offer solutions.

PERSONAL ENTREPRENEURIAL SPACE

The combination of the three components – talent, passion and external need – creates a creative psychological space that we at The-Hub named the Personal Entrepreneurial Space (PES). Everyone has PES, and it can be discovered and nurtured through coaching. There is nothing more fulfilling than helping people realize their PES and act upon it. The-Hub was designed to provide exactly this kind of support.

When people begin to act from their PES, they often encounter a series of barriers and fears. These include the fear of failure, the personal and family costs of devoting most of their energy to the project, and the challenge of leaving a comfortable and familiar reality, often referred to as the comfort zone. They start hearing voices from their close and distant environment warning them about the risks and predicting failure, often without any basis in fact.

In these moments, people need to listen to their inner voice and believe in the combination of talent, need and passion. By harnessing one's personal talent and passion to work on a solution to a real need in the community and the world, the entrepreneur practices a higher level of personal participation in the greater good – an authentic contribution that benefits both self and society.

THE TREND OF HUBS

While nurturing each individual's Personal Entrepreneurial Space (PES) was at the heart of our mission, it became clear that the broader trend of shared workspaces was rapidly evolving around us. One aspect we didn't emphasize enough was The-Hub's business model. While we focused on the social significance of the venture and its contribution to society, others worldwide recognized the enormous potential of shared workspaces. Gradually, competing shared workspaces emerged globally, treating the concept primarily as a real estate venture and crafting business plans based on maximizing every square meter. This trend did not skip Tel Aviv, and soon, after about two years of operating almost alone in the arena, commercial shared workspaces like WeWork, MindSpace and others began to appear. Today, there are 102 shared workspaces in Tel Aviv, rendering The-Hub less relevant.

However, we were among the first to identify a significant trend that will not disappear but will only continue to develop. The phenomenon of shared workspaces is crucial in our discussion on people's need to belong alongside their need to express and act from their uniqueness. Hubs of various kinds are seemingly the ultimate structure for this purpose: on the one hand, every individual or team is engaged in their venture and thus in their personal expression. On the other hand, the need to be together and feel part of a community is well met in such places. Community managers and hosts in shared workspaces invest heavily in creating a community and a sense of belonging. They do so because the clients are not obligated to stay long-term, and they know that the more clients feel at home, the more likely they are to remain. The clients, in turn, receive a smaller personal space than they would if they rented separate offices at the same price. Despite this, they enjoy the opportunity to leave isolation, meet people, consult, collaborate, identify business opportunities and feel part of a community.

Hubs will continue to be a sought-after phenomenon, especially in light of the rise in remote work and the increased demand for freelancers. People who work remotely and provide services as freelancers look for places to work from, so they don't have to travel far from their homes but also don't want to be confined to their homes. Despite the advantages of working from home, there are many distractions, loneliness, difficulty maintaining self-discipline and more. Regional hubs are gaining momentum as a solution for freelancers and creative people who want to realize themselves while yearning for connection and community.

'HUBS' AS A SOLUTION FOR MARGINALIZED POPULATIONS – THE CASE OF 'LOTUS'

Hubs are not just a solution for freelancers. There are entire communities that, for religious, traditional or other functional reasons, cannot leave their place of residence to travel to distant workplaces. I was involved in the establishment of a very unique hub, entirely the initiative and vision of Maysa, a Druze entrepreneur from the village of Usfiya on Mount Carmel near Haifa. Maysa came to my office one day for a meeting about her vision. I saw an impressive woman, dressed in the traditional religious attire of the Druze community. The moment she started talking about her vision, her eyes lit up, her face beamed, and I felt that I was facing a true leader.

She told me about the reality experienced by religious Druze women. For religious reasons, they cannot pursue higher education, are not allowed to learn to drive and are not permitted to leave the village. Therefore, although many of them study in high school in scientific tracks and excel in their studies, they are not able to continue studying or develop a significant career that matches their intellectual level. Many of them find temporary jobs in the village, with very low wages and without any self-fulfillment. Maysa envisioned how these women could learn computer programming and start working for high-tech companies that would employ them remotely.

When she came to my office, the dream was very high-level, and it was necessary to build it from the ground up, much like a startup (see the diagram, below, that we prepared together at that meeting. It is in Hebrew, but you can easily get it).

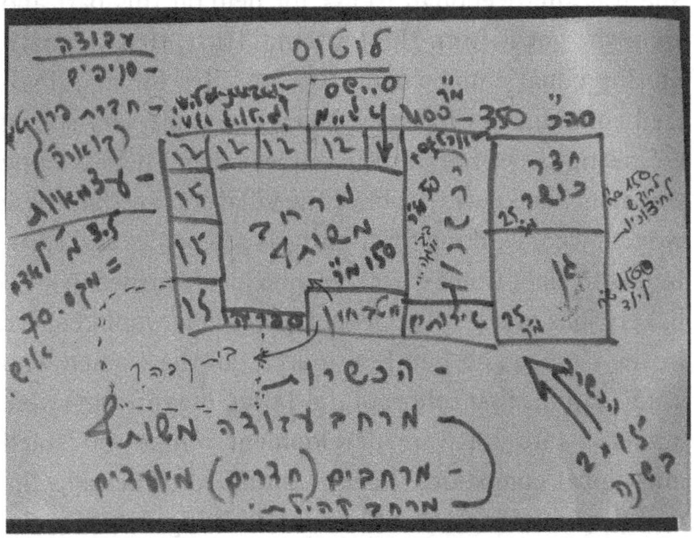

A sketch of a dream on a napkin.
(Photo: Danny Gal.)

The path to the dream had many challenges, including gaining the agreement of the village's religious leaders, finding a suitable training program, finding a place for the training, working with the women on the necessary mental – not just technical – shift and more. Maysa did not shy away from any challenge or obstacle and led the project with a firm hand until everyone was convinced. Initially, the religious leaders were skeptical, as were the local authority and leadership. But when Maysa managed to find sponsors and commercial money started flowing into the village, everyone increased their belief and support in the program.

Maysa knew that the key to the program's success was finding employers willing to hire the women remotely. She was smart enough to ask for help on this part and soon she got it from the Portland Trust, that was promoting equal employment opportunities for marginalized communities in Israel. They had some very strong connections with high-tech employers and helped bring them on. She knew that once the villagers saw that these women were working for high-tech companies and earning six to eight times what they previously earned in local bakery jobs or as house cleaners, everyone would believe in the change and join her. Indeed, all the women who studied in the first cohort of the 'Lotus' organization were accepted into software development centers of Israeli and global companies. Maysa continued to develop the vision and, alongside additional training cohorts, she established a magnificent hub in the village, including a training center, a remote work center, and other support centers for working women and their needs as mothers. Maysa's vision came true and opened possibilities for many more women to try to fulfill their dreams.

The first training cohort of the 'Lotus' women's organization,
The participants' faces are hidden to protect their privacy.
(Photo: Danny Gal.)

'Lotus' is an excellent example of the phenomenon of local and regional hubs that provide a solution for people who could not work remotely before. As remote work trends continue, the demand for such places will increase. Then the question will arise: What is the dominant organizational identity and affiliation of workers in these hubs? Will the affiliation with the hub become leading, or will the connection with the remote employer still be the most significant work relationship? This is a challenge that organizations must address, and perhaps even build joint strategies with organizations offering hubs to coordinate and synchronize actions in a way that preserves the interests of all players: the organization, the hub and the employee (including their family and community). A further discussion on the question of organizational culture in the era of remote work can be found in the section on the post-COVID world of work.

Most of the organizations have a more traditional structure than The-Hub and the challenge is how to import this spirit to regular organizations – how to create a culture in which each individual is encouraged to find their PES and be involved in creating something meaningful and not just in task execution. I know this is possible not only for knowledge workers but for all kinds of workers. Even sanitation workers can be treated in a way that will be appreciative and encourage them to solve municipal problems and improve the quality of life of the community in which they work. In some places, the sanitation workers are actually sustainability ambassadors or recycling artists. It is just a matter of awareness and intention to add meaning and self-expression to each worker in each industry.

While understanding and managing otherness within organizations can help create inclusive environments, the broader question remains: How can empathy play a role in resolving conflicts that extend beyond the workplace, particularly in global contexts? In the next chapter, we will explore how empathy, or the lack thereof, shapes the dynamics of large-scale conflicts and impacts our ability to find common ground amid division.

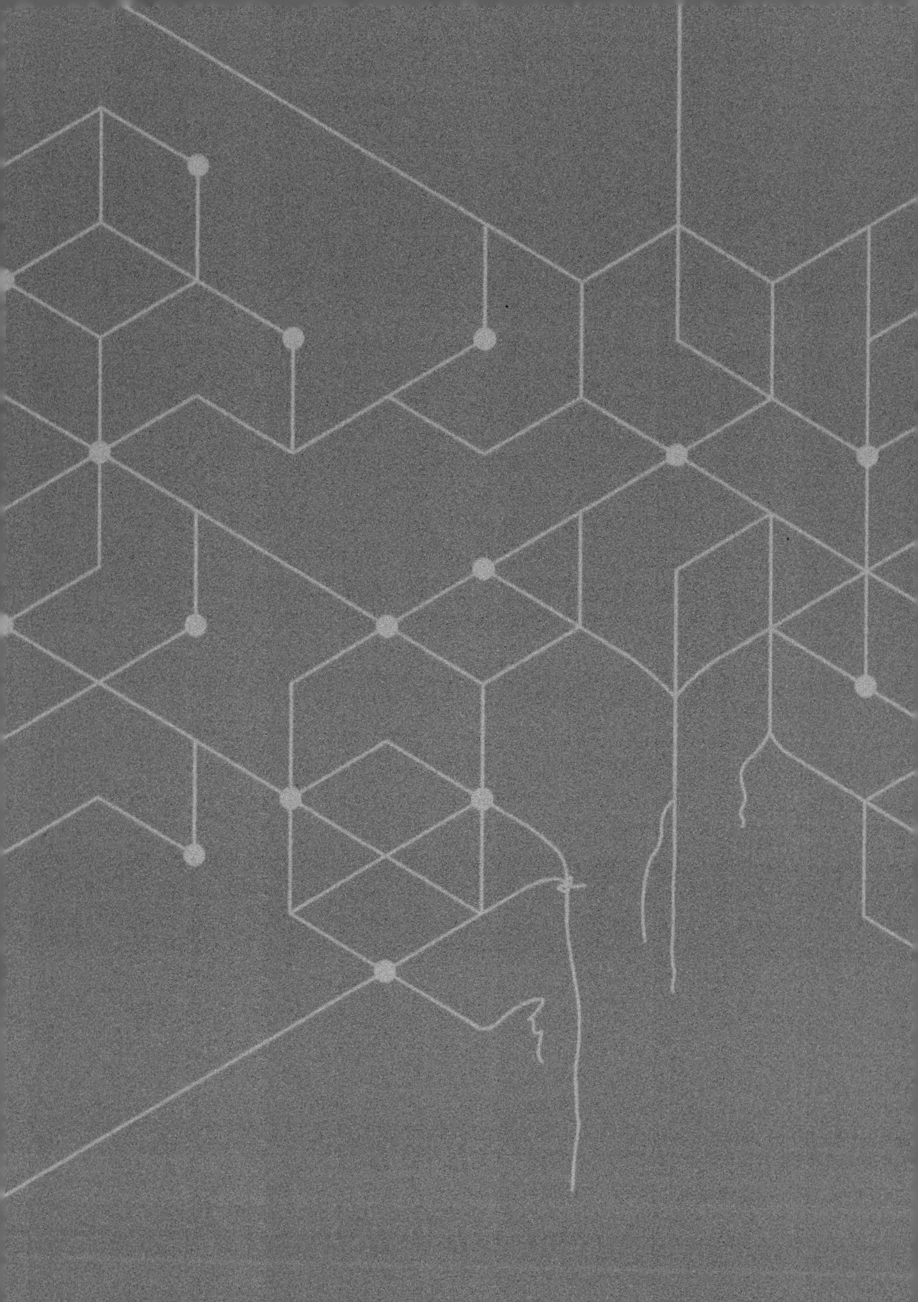

CHAPTER 12

GLOBAL CONFLICTS AND THE CRISIS OF EMPATHY

In today's world, numerous conflicts persist, such as the Russia-Ukraine war, the Israeli-Palestinian conflict, and less-visible African conflicts like those in Sudan (between the Sudanese Armed Forces and the Rapid Support Forces) and the Democratic Republic of Congo. These conflicts are sustained by a variety of factors, including historical grievances, economic pressures, international power dynamics and cultural clashes.

However, another crucial perspective, which I suggest in our discussion, is that many of these conflicts, whether large-scale wars or regional tensions, are fundamentally driven by a basic failure of empathy, as discussed earlier. Each side clings to the belief that it holds the absolute truth, remaining blind to the suffering of the other. This suffering is often manipulated and transformed into political power by leaders who portray themselves as protectors of their people. In reality, these leaders perpetuate and intensify the conflict to maintain their grip on power.

Understanding this dynamic is crucial for overcoming intractable conflicts. Being empathetic toward the other side doesn't mean betraying your loyalty to your own. True empathy involves recognizing and standing firm in your own identity and values while also understanding the perspective of the other side. This understanding can be purely cognitive, or it can involve opening your heart. When this balance is achieved, a scaffold is created that may lay the foundations for a bridge of understanding.

Through these lenses, I would like to share stories and conclusions from my work in the Israeli-Palestinian conflict, where fostering empathy and understanding between adversaries has been a central goal. The experiences I will be sharing occurred before the current Israel-Hamas conflict that began on 7 October 2023. However, the principles and ideas remain highly relevant.

DIFFERENT BACKGROUNDS, SHARED DREAMS

I was born and raised in Israel in a very patriotic atmosphere. I was educated in Israeli schools that celebrate the Israeli independence and glorify the heroes of wars that protected our country. At the age of 18, I joined the Israeli Defence Forces (IDF) and carried out my duty. As I grew up, I was more aware of the conflict between Israel and the Palestinians and understood that this was the most burning issue that needed to be solved if we wanted to have a safe future as an independent state. I felt like I had a duty to work on peace building that was not less important than my army service, maybe even more. I was fortunate to have a set of tools that I used as an organizational consultant in other settings, and I felt I should bring them with me to the building bridges activity.

With that intention in mind, I looked for opportunities to meet with Palestinians like me and discuss what could be done. This led me to a meeting between Israelis and Palestinians organized by three partners: an Israeli named Yitzhak, a Palestinian named Zoughbi, and an American named Whit. The meeting was held at a hotel in Beit Jala, near Jerusalem, at a place where the separation wall had not yet been built: the Everest Hotel. The callers of the meeting were smart enough to invite a few foreign facilitators: Toke, Sarah and Maria who used a method called 'The Art of Hosting' to deal with the sensitivities in the room. My experience of the meeting was mind- and heart-blowing. I felt such strong emotions that I could hardly contain them. My body knew before my mind that I had found my calling. The opportunity to sit with someone who, until that moment, I perceived as an 'enemy,' to face the fear and overcome it – I felt something special was happening and I fully committed myself to the meeting.

One of the tasks in the meeting was to sit with a partner from the other side and interview each other about life, focusing on the small details of daily life. Additionally, each person had to say something about their dreams. I sat with a Palestinian woman named Sawsan from the Palestinian city of Hebron. Sawsan and I were about the same age. She told me a very familiar story about the challenges of raising children, educational dilemmas, the pressure to find suitable employment, and paying off loans. I told her my story, and we were surprised to hear how similar our stories were despite the (imagined) mental distance between us. It was the first time I sat down and got to know a Palestinian person deeply, eye to eye, not someone who came to provide a service or seek work in Israel. It was a very special feeling, different from what I expected. I felt a connection between us. The feeling only grew stronger when we realized our dreams were strikingly similar: to sit on the beach in Tel Aviv, eat watermelon and watch our children play in the sand. We could even fantasize about gathering with our families on the Tel Aviv beach, sharing these simple yet profound moments together.

However, the reality was (and still is) that only my family could live this dream, while Sawsan's family was prevented from reaching the beach from the Palestinian territory. The disparity between the dream and reality shook me deeply, making me realize how profound and pervasive my disconnection from the Palestinian population living next to us truly was.

Our story was later shared with all the seminar participants, who resonated with and echoed similar experiences. Within a few hours of joint activities, a unique atmosphere of human connection emerged in the seminar space, transcending stereotypes, language barriers and cultural differences. The personal connections forged were more powerful than any political discussion I had ever participated in. This experience illuminated the path I wanted to pursue: fostering connections between human beings, beyond opinions and political agenda, especially in conflict situations.

DIALOGUE BETWEEN ENEMIES

Fortunately, the meeting organizers noticed the sense of purpose that emerged in me from the experience and reached out to me. After the meeting, I received an invitation to participate in a global gathering of social activists in Canada to share the Israeli perspective on the Israeli-Palestinian conflict. Ibrahim, a Palestinian school principal who also attended the meeting, received the same invitation. The intention was for Ibrahim and me to participate in the conference and undergo training to continue facilitating these meetings between Israelis and Palestinians and establish an organization around this initiative.

Unfortunately, Ibrahim couldn't attend the meeting due to permit issues and visa denial, a common obstacle for Palestinians wishing to travel abroad. Despite this setback, my participation in the meeting and the connection with Ibrahim led us, under the leadership of Dr. Whit Jones from the US, to establish the Center for Emerging Futures (CEF). Through this organization, we have held dozens of seminars between Israelis and Palestinians. These meetings have provided participants with hope and, in many cases, fundamentally changed their perceptions of 'the other.'

MANAGING CONFLICT MEETINGS

The meetings followed the same method I experienced in my first encounter: 'The Art of Hosting,' developed by several organizational consultants in Europe and the US. This method has been successfully implemented in places requiring leadership to solve tough community problems and co-design better futures.

Before each meeting, a planning process was conducted with a team of Israeli-Palestinian facilitators. They discussed the unique theme for each meeting and jointly formulated the invitation. The more precise the invitation, the more suitable the participants, as they arrived with the right expectations. Typically, the invitation read something like:

"You are invited to a meeting where we will get to know each other as human beings, beyond politics, stereotypes and fears, and explore our dreams for a potential shared future."

This approach attracted people from all backgrounds, not just peace activists and regular participants in such meetings. It drew in individuals curious about understanding the other side, often coming with many hesitations and sensitivities.

I remember that many Israelis feared arriving because the meeting was held in Palestinian territory. For many Israelis, traveling to Palestinian territories and staying in a Palestinian hotel involved confronting fears and stepping sharply out of their comfort zone. The fears were similar on the Palestinian side, who experienced difficulties in reaching the meeting, adding to the tension participants felt upon arrival. Palestinians came from various parts of the West Bank and Gaza Strip. The journey, often by public transportation, involved passing through several checkpoints, waiting in long lines, undergoing security checks, and sometimes even confrontations with Israeli security forces. Therefore, the starting conditions for the meetings were emotionally charged, with a lot of fear and negative thoughts about the other side.

Each meeting was attended by approximately 50–60 people, including around 20–25 Israelis, 20–25 Palestinians, and five to ten individuals from other parts of the world who were curious and interested in the conflict-and-facilitation method. The presence of the international participants was critical. They provided a sense of neutrality and significantly contributed to everyone's feeling of security. Without prior planning, the role played by the internationals was not that of mediators, assistants or supporters of one side or the other. Instead, they participated as equals, fully engaging in all activities and feeling that, whether they wanted to or not, they were part of the solution by just being present, genuinely curious and not taking sides. The meeting was not just a private matter for Israelis and Palestinians. All sides felt that others cared about them and were willing to be part of the long journey toward collective healing.

Once participants arrived at the hotel, they were met with a welcoming, festive atmosphere disconnected from the outside reality, allowing them to settle in, breathe and enter a different mindset.

Significant thought was given to the design of the meeting space. It was important for us to plan the meetings to convey equality, humanity and attentiveness. The room was arranged in a single large circle of chairs, with a small, decorated table in the center, holding several items that the facilitators would use later.

The opening circle.

LISTENING CIRCLES

Each meeting began with a listening circle, where each participant, in turn, was asked to introduce themself, share how their journey to the meeting was, and why they chose to come. The facilitators used a 'talking piece' that passed around the circle to focus the listening on the speaker and allow everyone to listen without needing to respond. From the very beginning, people began to share very personal and moving things, and the room filled with deep listening and empathy. The listening process took time as each speaker spoke in their preferred language (Arabic/Hebrew/English) and their words were immediately translated into the other languages. The slowness in this case added to the sense of listening and made it clear to the participants that they had come to a place where people were truly interested in them and saw them, with all the baggage they brought to the meeting.

Participants shared events that happened to them on the way to the meeting, including fears of coming, traumas they carried from the past, and the great excitement of coming to such a space and meeting the other side for the first time. Some shed tears, and some kept a certain distance to see where all this would lead. The round continued until the last speaker. It ended with the facilitators acknowledging the listening atmosphere in the room, the variety of stories people brought, and the attention to the fact that everyone who came here did so with curiosity and openness to meet the other and perhaps even challenge some of their original thoughts about the other.

The listening circle is an ancient tradition used in ancient tribes that allowed a group of people to have a conversation and make joint decisions. There are facilitation methods that have adopted these traditions and adapted them to our times. The circle creates an egalitarian structure without hierarchy. The talking piece allows each person to have a voice. The circle enables everyone to belong and choose how to present themselves. This structure prevents the instinct of many to react to what they hear and engage in arguments. It slows down the pace and provides an opportunity to hear, see and listen to the bigger picture, the unspoken words, the music and the energy.

On the other hand, the circle is also an exposed structure where everyone can see each other, which can be challenging and even intimidating for some people. The role of the facilitator is to make it legitimate to stay silent until someone is ready to speak. The circle practice keeps everyone focused, it is inclusive by nature, calming down, and sets the quality of listening for the whole weekend.

FACING FEAR: THE TRANSFORMATIVE POWER OF LISTENING

I have facilitated many listening circles within the context of these CEF seminars. In one circle that I remember particularly well, I heard a disturbing story from one of the participants. The speaker, a Palestinian from a refugee camp in the West Bank, recounted how his brother's close friend was shot and killed by an Israeli sniper on his way home from school. The speaker's brother, who was with his friend at the time, was traumatized by the incident, leading him to sink into depression, isolate himself and eventually connect with militant groups who intended for him to become a suicide bomber as an act of revenge. Tragically, the young man carried out the suicide bombing on a bus in Jerusalem, resulting in the loss of innocent civilian lives. At the time, the speaker was an ambulance driver. After the incident, he left his job and became a mentor for street gangs and unemployed youths to prevent them from going down the same path as his brother.

His story shocked everyone and threatened to unravel the circle. Fortunately, everyone took a deep breath and allowed the listening process to continue. Immediately after the round ended, I chose to approach this person and have an in-depth conversation about the story he just shared. This was not an easy move; the thought of sitting with the brother of a suicide bomber unsettled me. However, the genuine intention in his voice to seek change and prevent future incidents intrigued me.

During our conversation, we got to know each other better, and I learned more details about his story. I thanked him for choosing to join our meeting and for his efforts to prevent similar incidents in the future. I felt that this space was important for him to validate his actions and engage with the other side, which had been deeply affected by his brother's act of terror. For me, it was an opportunity to test the limits of my listening and empathy. Was there anyone I couldn't sit with and listen to? Was turning my back on those who frightened me the right strategy?

Could I connect with and face those I feared? These were real challenges. Although the person I was speaking with was not the terrorist, it was both a shocking and necessary moment for me.

THE CHALLENGE OF LISTENING TO EMOTIONALLY CHARGED CONTENT

This conversation was part of the activity that followed the initial listening circle. Participants were instructed to pair up with someone from the circle who drew their curiosity and was not from their ethnic group. The task was to interview each other and try to listen to personal stories and shared dreams, much like I did with Sawsan during my first meeting as a participant.

I observed several phenomena during these conversations. When people shared difficult experiences resulting from the conflict, it often created a very uncomfortable situation for the listener. In some cases, the listener felt the need to ask the speaker questions to understand why the incident happened and what role (if any) they played in it. For example, when people from Gaza shared about the hardships of life there, the listener felt compelled to ask, "But why did you vote for Hamas and allow them to take over Gaza in democratic elections?" There was a difficulty in simply listening without trying to understand the cause of the situation or pointing fingers at who was responsible. In other cases, the response to difficult stories was the opposite:

the listener felt guilt and responsibility for what had happened, even though they were not involved in the event.

In both cases, the listening was limited to the downloading type of listening (as explained in chapter 2). When the story being told was painful and difficult, the listener found it hard to just listen and acknowledge the pain without trying to find someone to blame or taking responsibility and feeling guilt for what happened. This phenomenon shows a kind of listening that internalizes the story and fails to separate the speaker's story from the listener. As a result, the listener feels the need to protect themselves or listen selectively and try to prove their own point. This, of course, does not support the speaker and does not allow them to experience a sense of empathy and understanding of their situation.

HOW TO PRACTICE EMPATHIC LISTENING IN CONFLICT SITUATIONS

Similar situations occur daily among close people such as life partners, family members, children and parents. One side shares a difficult experience, hoping for empathy. Instead, the listener feels the need to respond with judgment (e.g., "Why did you do that?"), excessive concern ("Are you okay? I'm so worried about you") or patronizing advice ("Next time, don't do that"). An empathetic response requires first listening without reacting. This means absorbing the message and trying to feel what the storyteller is experiencing.

From this empathetic listening, one can reflect back what was heard to ensure understanding (e.g., "I hear that a kid was bullying you at school, and it's the same kid who has been bullying you recently"), and then resonate with an empathetic feeling such as, "That must have been very hard for you." The more the storyteller feels heard and seen in their distress, the more their need for empathy will be met, allowing them to begin recovering.

The principle suggested here, which worked very well in Israeli-Palestinian meetings and can be applied in any situation, is: Listen, notice, acknowledge and empathize – without blaming or taking excessive responsibility for the situation.

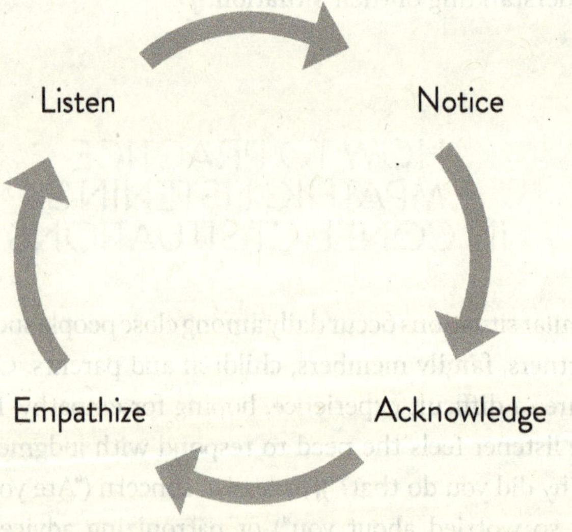

In Chapter 12, we have explored the role of empathy – or its absence – in fueling and resolving global conflicts, touching on the Israeli-Palestinian conflict as one of many examples. In the next chapter, we will take a deeper dive into a specific, recent instance: the Israel-Gaza crisis of October 2023. Through my personal account, I aim to share the emotional complexities and challenges of empathy during times of war, and what lessons we can draw about navigating conflict amid personal and collective trauma.

CHAPTER 13

EMPATHY AMID CONFLICT: LESSONS FROM THE ISRAEL-GAZA CRISIS

The story I am about to share is told from the perspective of an Israeli who was in Israel when unfortunate events began on 7 October 2023. It might be biased toward the Israeli viewpoint as I experienced the events first-hand, but my intention in this book is to convey a balanced message, not to make a political statement. Please read with patience, as I will also try to practice seeing things from the other side. There are no winners in wars, only losers. The scale of the catastrophe on both sides is devastating. But there is also hope.

On 7 October 2023, at 6:30 am, Israel woke up to a nightmare. Thousands of Hamas terrorists from Gaza infiltrated Israel, occupying villages and cities near the Israel-Gaza border. They massacred, raped and kidnapped innocent civilians, resulting in the brutal deaths of approximately 1,500 Israelis. The horrific nature of these acts serves as a stark reminder to humanity that such cruelty still exists.

To illustrate the scale of this tragedy from an Israeli perspective, consider the impact of the 9/11 attacks in the US, but multiplied by 14, given Israel's population of just 10 million. This event has had, and continues to have, a profound effect on Israel, reviving Holocaust trauma for many Israelis and Jewish people worldwide.

On 8 October, my 12-year-old daughter, witnessing her parents almost paralyzed by fear, asked me, "Dad, is this as big as the Holocaust?" I had to explain that it wasn't nearly as devastating, but from the perspective of a 12-year-old, it seemed just as terrifying. We made every effort, though with limited success, to protect her from the full extent of the horror by filtering what she watched and heard from media sources. But for us adults, it was and still is a nightmare.

Apart from our shock and fear from the massacre committed by Hamas, we were also shocked by the absence and inability of the Israeli Defence Forces (IDF) to stop Hamas on the first day of the attack. We always counted on the IDF to protect us, and when this didn't happen, we were deeply disappointed, and our full trust in the army was cracked.

Indeed, the IDF were unprepared, exhibiting arrogance and overconfidence in believing that such an attack could never occur. Hundreds of people were kidnapped and held as hostages in Gaza, plunging Israeli society into a state of shock. Despite the bloody history of the state since its establishment in 1948, such an event had never happened in Israel before.

To illustrate the profound impact this situation had on me, as it did on many others, I will share that for the first time since my army service 25 years ago, I applied for a weapon permit to protect my family.

The Israeli government felt it had no choice but to declare war against Hamas in Gaza. Despite the government being at a low point in terms of public trust, there was initially widespread support for this action within Israel and much of the global community. It was seen as a justified response to the attacks carried out by Hamas on 7 October.

But Hamas had prepared for a long time by digging tunnels, accumulating ammunition and hiding under civilian hospitals, mosques and dense neighborhoods. The IDF had to use a lot of force to start destroying Hamas' infrastructure and military capabilities, and this had an enormous collateral impact. Large parts of Gaza were destroyed and more than 35,000 Gazans were killed, including many civilians, children, women and other uninvolved people. The situation quickly deteriorated into a regional catastrophe of unprecedented proportions. The suffering of the Gazan people was beyond imagination.

As I mentioned earlier, this book will not delve deeply into the political implications of the conflict. However, it is important to note that I am part of a group of Israelis who have spent years working to build bridges and achieve a peaceful resolution for both sides. From this perspective, I am acutely aware that the 7 October 2023 outburst is an extraordinary event in the long chain of unfortunate incidents in the Israeli-Palestinian conflict, which has lasted for over 50 years. This current war represents a significant setback, and it feels as though many people on both sides, including peace activists, are losing hope that this conflict will ever be resolved. Personally, I continue to hold onto a sliver of hope, keeping my heart open to the possibility that something positive might emerge from the destruction.

THE EMPATHY CRISIS

I would like to address these events through the lens of the empathy crisis and the inability of people to see each other's suffering, especially when they feel like victims themselves. To illustrate this, I will share a personal story from our small kibbutz, a communal village in the mid-north of Israel. Since 7 October, the southern and northern parts of Israel were evacuated due to constant fire from Gaza in the south and Lebanon (Hezbollah) in the north. Similarly, 1.5 million Gazans and thousands of southern Lebanese citizens faced evacuations. Fortunately, my kibbutz was not on the front line, allowing us to continue with a semi-routine life, although we remained very alert and frightened by the unfolding conflict. Some of us had to rejoin the army as reservists, while those who stayed behind helped maintain routine life in the kibbutz.

As the situation escalated and we mourned everything that happened on 7 October, we began to hear more about the growing numbers of people killed and injured on the Gazan side. The numbers grew to an unbelievable scale, making it hard to comprehend the extent of destruction and suffering on the other side. The media in Israel didn't help; TV panels were dominated by ex-generals commenting with a militaristic perspective, leaving no room for doubt. "We must retaliate," they said, "and restore our deterrent power at all costs." It was almost as if revenge was a legitimate strategy, and I even heard one ex-general explicitly say so in a broadcast.

The media collaborated with the patriotic tone and showed very little of what was happening in Gaza.

However, I went online to Arabic news agencies like Al-Jazeera and Al-Arabia to check the situation for myself. What I found was horrifying, and I couldn't justify it to myself, even though I knew we had to stop Hamas from ever being able to repeat this attack. It felt like a deadlock situation. It was clear that some ministers in the Israeli government were seeking revenge, whereas other moderate leaders in Israel were ready to examine other strategies. Being a leader requires a sense of responsibility and strategic thinking even in the most difficult situations.

One possible strategy to help in such situations is building an international coalition to support Israel in achieving its goals while avoiding the collateral destruction of Gaza. Similar coalitions have been established in the past, such as during the First Gulf War, when Secretary Baker successfully formed a coalition that included Arab countries like Egypt and Jordan to counter Iraq's aggression under Saddam Hussein, who had occupied Kuwait. Opportunities for such coalitions likely exist again. Revenge should not be a driving force; leaders must be strong enough to face public anger and remain calm when making decisions. Unfortunately, the government, acting in full alignment with public sentiment, initiated the longest and bloodiest war in Israel's history, ultimately failing to achieve its declared goals of destroying Hamas and returning the hostages.

The pain and sorrow Israelis felt united them in the first few months of the war but also blocked any opportunity to feel empathy for the other side that was under a huge attack. When I tried to share my concern about the suffering of uninvolved and innocent Gazan civilians with friends, I was surprised by their reaction. They were angry at me: "How can you think of the Gazans after what they did to us? Didn't you see the videos of the massacre? Didn't you see the citizens of Gaza celebrating in the streets after those bloody acts by Hamas? Don't you think they would do it again if they could?" I tried to explain that I was as shocked as they were by what happened on 7 October, but that it didn't give us the mandate to act in the same way, and that we must stop the suffering of uninvolved people. It was a dead-end conversation. They didn't want to listen. In fact, they were furious at me, and some have kept their distance from me since then.

A NEW INSIGHT ABOUT EMPATHY

I had to stop expressing my thoughts and feelings on this matter with my neighbors. While I continued to voice my concerns on social media and in civil demonstrations against the government's policy, I realized there was something crucial to learn about the capacity for empathy in such situations. When someone is hurt, it's difficult to expect them to open their hearts. The instinct is to be defensive and protect oneself, like a hedgehog. However, the mind should still be able to function. There is a difference between cognitive empathy – understanding the other side's perspective – and emotional empathy – feeling the other side's suffering. Sometimes it is more realistic to expect cognitive empathy rather than emotional empathy. Nonetheless, we shouldn't accept a situation where we are completely blind to the other side's suffering, even if they have done terrible things to us. That can lead to disastrous results.

One of the reasons it is difficult to practice empathy in such extreme situations is our tendency to generalize and stereotype those who hurt us, viewing them as a single homogenous group. This makes it difficult to differentiate between murderous terrorists and regular citizens who, even if they hold hatred, are unarmed and do not pose an immediate threat. Such stereotyping demonizes the other side, giving a perceived permission to hunt the demon until it is destroyed.

I can understand why many Gazans hate us, given their years of living under siege in one of the densest and poorest areas in the world. Before the war, a Gazan person couldn't travel outside Gaza, couldn't study abroad, and couldn't trade or import goods like we can. As I said earlier, I will not delve into the political context that caused this situation, but from a civilian perspective, it is one of the worst places to live in the world. Anyone outside of Israel reading this may immediately empathize with the Gazans. However, Israelis who were directly hurt find it difficult to empathize, and it will take years to recover this capacity.

Make no mistake, I support the effort to disarm Hamas and ensure they are out of power in Gaza, never again threatening Israel. However, I don't believe we should destroy Gaza and kill so many uninvolved people. We must act out of a commitment to protect our people while also using restrained force that considers the suffering on the other side.

This story reminds me of the fragile nature of empathy. Even the most compassionate and empathetic individuals can become rigid and militant when they feel personally hurt. The hardest thing in the world is to feel empathy for those who have attacked you. The natural tendency is to focus on your own wounds and fight back. When fighting back, it is hard to find softness within yourself. Empathy for the other side stops when the heart is injured and bleeding by the same side that should be the recipient of your empathy.

TOWARD A NEW DEMOCRACY: EMBRACING DIVERSITY AND INCLUSION

The current crisis will eventually calm down, and the winds of war will be replaced by the vibrant forces of the economy, culture, education and other life mechanisms on both sides. The wounds and exposed nerves will undergo a healing and rehabilitation process, allowing societies to return to a calmer state. However, new, deep scars have formed, and many people find it difficult to trust the other side. A new collective trauma has been created, adding to past traumas for both people.

This is similar to other regions that have experienced the horrors of war, like Ukraine and Russia, the former states of Yugoslavia, and even American society with its history of enslavement and injustice against Black people. The wounds are still open and, from time to time, these undercurrents erupt, as seen in painful cases like the killing of Eric Garner by a police officer in 2014 ("I can't breathe") and George Floyd's case in 2020 (a police officer knelt on his neck for over nine minutes), which led to the formation of the 'Black Lives Matter' movement in the US and around the world.

Societies will continue to live with diversity and mixed sets of interests and loyalties. Two forces will always be at work simultaneously: the force of life, which creates connections between diverse individuals in workplaces, hospitals, markets, construction sites, football fields and music clubs; and the force of fear, distrust and demonization of the 'other,' along with the constant reminder that things could flare up again at any moment, threatening unity. This duality is deeply rooted in the idea of a shared society, one composed of different subcultures and various population groups. The challenge is to create a common fabric where everyone feels they belong to something greater than themselves while remaining true to their original identity and traditions without needing to hide, feel ashamed or be afraid.

In the past, this was a unique challenge for Israel and other countries with mixed populations from different ethnic backgrounds. In today's world, in the third decade of the millennium, this is no longer just the situation in countries like Israel. Waves of refugees are flooding developed countries, populations are becoming increasingly mixed everywhere, and the need to learn to live together is becoming a local and existential issue, not just distant news from troubled regions.

Historically, democracies were not designed to protect the rights of minorities. Ancient democratic systems, like those in Athens and Rome, were exclusive, allowing only privileged groups to participate while excluding women, slaves and noncitizens.

Today's democracies must continue to evolve, shifting from a majority-rule principle to one that ensures fair representation and protection for all individuals, including minorities. This evolution is crucial for maintaining a balanced and equitable society.

In the United States, modern democracy initially tolerated slavery and discrimination against Black people. The US democracy evolved over time, gradually expanding rights through struggles such as the Civil Rights Movement. However, the original intent of the democratic framework did not prioritize the rights of minorities.

In the United States, whites are projected to become a minority compared to other ethnic groups (Hispanics, Blacks, Asians, Native Americans and others) by 2045. In Israel, non-ultra-Orthodox Jews are expected to become a minority compared to the combined ultra-Orthodox and Arab populations by 2065. In Europe, the Muslim population is projected to grow significantly, potentially reaching up to 14% of the total population by 2050 under high migration scenarios.

These changes necessitate a profound and fundamental shift in the democratic system. The central principle must transition from a simple majority rule to a more inclusive framework that ensures every group's needs are heard and addressed. This includes mechanisms like proportional representation, participatory budgeting and citizens' assemblies, which allow diverse voices to influence public policy.

Moreover, the democratic process should empower all individuals to participate actively and see how their contributions shape society. Educational initiatives to promote civic engagement and platforms for public discourse can help achieve this.

Additionally, it is crucial that judicial systems, such as the supreme courts in democratic countries, maintain their power to check and balance governmental policies. These institutions must safeguard human rights and protect minorities from potential abuses of power. Ensuring judicial independence and reinforcing legal protections for minority groups are essential steps in this direction.

By implementing these changes, democracies can better navigate demographic shifts and foster a more inclusive and equitable society.

One opportunity to experience this new type of democracy was through an experiment I co-initiated during the social protests of 2011. In the next chapter, I will tell the story of this experiment, drawing compelling conclusions about its impact and its potential for shaping the future of democratic engagement.

As we reflect on the crises that test our empathy, it becomes clear that the need for a more inclusive and participatory approach to resolving conflicts has never been greater. In the next chapter, we explore an inspiring experiment that took place during a time of social upheaval – a potential glimpse into a new type of democracy that could foster belonging and connection in divided societies.

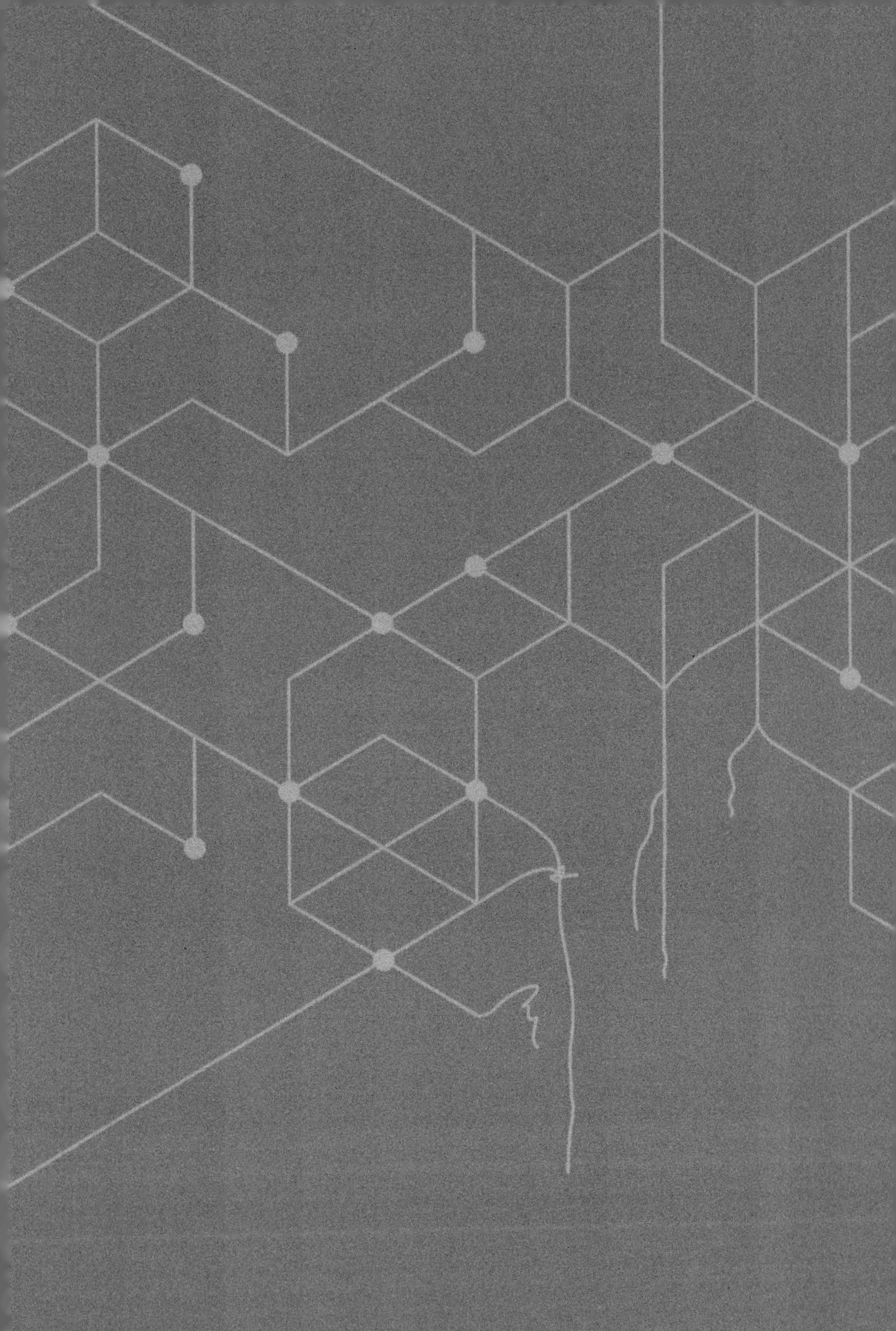

CHAPTER 14

A POTENTIAL NEW DEMOCRACY OF BELONGING

One way to overcome conflicts that tear society apart is to find a unifying issue around which different groups can organize. This happened in the summer of 2011. It began in Tunisia on 17 December 2010, when the late Mohamed Bouazizi, a street vendor, set himself on fire in protest against the authorities' arbitrariness and the regime's corruption. Bouazizi's act sparked a wave of massive protests in Tunisia and subsequently ignited the Middle East in Egypt, Algeria, Libya, Yemen, Syria and more, in a period known as the 'Arab Spring.' This movement inspired mass social protests in other countries in Europe, including Spain, Greece, England, and later in the United States (Occupy Wall Street). The common outcry of all the protesters was the desire for social justice. The protesters were fed up with a situation in which 1% of the world's population holds wealth equivalent to 50% of the global wealth. In the US, for example, three individuals hold more wealth than the bottom 50% of the US population.

THE BIRTH OF THE PROTEST IN ISRAEL

In the summer of 2011, the protest spread to Israel when Daphni Leef, an anonymous woman up until that time, moved into a tent on Rothschild Boulevard after her landlord decided to unilaterally raise her rent. Daphni invited a few friends, who invited more friends, and within a few days, the protest grew exponentially, sweeping almost the entire country into the largest social struggle in Israel's history. "The people demand social justice" was the cry at the massive demonstrations organized week after week. The atmosphere in the country was new and unfamiliar: people who usually disagreed on controversial issues united around the demand for social justice and demonstrated together as if there was only one problem in the world. A kind of solidarity was created among diverse individuals in the united demand for "social justice."

THE 'THOUSAND ROUND TABLES' PROJECT

During this time, I had the opportunity to host Daphni Leef and her friends at The-Hub Tel Aviv, the social entrepreneurship incubator and co-working space I co-founded with my partner Eli on the roof of a Tel Aviv office building. Our place had been dealing with social disparities and finding creative solutions for a just and shared society for years before the 2011 protest. Therefore, it was only natural that when the protest broke out, The-Hub served as a home for the protest leaders and attracted many people trying to navigate and lead the protest. We, at The-Hub Tel Aviv, also felt a desire to contribute something to the collective effort. In the spirit of The-Hub, we thought the right thing to do would be to hold a public discussion on the question: What is the social justice we are demanding, and how can we achieve it?

At The-Hub, when we wanted to hold any community discussion, we would invite our entire community of entrepreneurs to a meeting using the World Café technique, started by Juanita Brown and David Isaacs (Brown J. 2005). In this method, participants are invited to exchange ideas around a specific topic and co-create a desired future. They sit around round tables and discuss a question around the topic. At the end of each discussion, they can move to another table, meet new people and discuss additional questions related to the central topic. After several rounds of discussions, the community begins to feel the shared insights and common themes. A common vision starts to form, and the participants are ready to think about how they can realize the ideas that emerged at the tables through personal and team initiatives.

In the midst of the social justice protest in Israel, we decided to step outside The-Hub's boundaries, set up several round tables on Rothschild Boulevard among the tents and invite the public to a discussion about social justice. The public's response was surprising and exciting. For three weeks, evening after evening, we held discussions with people who had their tent set in the boulevard or other visitors from all over Israel who came to support and witness the unprecedented event taking place during the protest. The conversations at the tables were exciting and fascinating. It showed how much people cared and how much they were proud to be Israelis in these days of social solidarity. Each meeting ended with the question: What would each of you like to take from here and initiate to make our lives better together? One evening, a young man named Assaf suggested, "Why don't we hold such roundtables all over the country?" When I heard his idea, I got goosebumps. I immediately saw the potential of the idea and believed in its feasibility. From that moment, the idea moved to rapid implementation.

A steering committee was established, consisting of top group facilitators, organizational consultants and media professionals. After a few days, we announced the '1000 Round Tables' initiative. It sounded crazy, but we believed we could invite 10,000 people to an enormous discussion about the future of Israeli society.

The date for the 1000 Round Tables event was set for 10 September 2011. It was a Saturday night, a week after the 'One Million Protest,' the largest demonstration of the social protest. The title we chose was: 'From Tent to Circle – 1000 Round Tables.' Participants were invited for 9pm across the country, with more than 30 sites where citizens gathered for a simultaneous discussion. The main event was in Tel Aviv, in the plaza in front of the Tel Aviv Museum of Art. By Saturday afternoon, the preparations were in full swing, and the square looked ready to accommodate thousands of citizens.

The plaza before the event.

By 9pm, there was no room left around the tables. Five thousand people in Tel Aviv and another 5,000 in other places around the country began the rounds of discussions. The response was amazing and immense. Each table had a facilitator, pre-briefed to hold a discussion where listening was the key element. Each facilitator had a documentation assistant with a laptop, capturing the main points discussed at the tables and emailing them to a central editing desk. The atmosphere in the square was almost sacred. The discussions created a pleasant hum of relaxed conversation, listening, mutual respect and a willingness to see and hear the other, even if they did not agree on everything. Everyone who participated in the event felt they were part of a historic moment, redefining what public participation could mean for shaping our shared lives and future.

The event in full swing.

THE DEMOCRACY THAT WANTS TO BE BORN

Everyone who participated in the event felt they were part of a historic moment, redefining what public participation could mean for shaping our shared lives and future. The democracy the world needs is a participatory democracy, where everyone has the opportunity, space and motivation to voice their unique perspective and influence. Referendums and elections have long ceased to be the main expression of democracy. In these events, there is so much fake news and misinformation that it is hard to achieve the results people truly intended. The future lies in local citizen participation in influencing their lives and choosing representatives they trust to represent them on larger issues at the national or global level. The roundtable event in 2011 was an early glimpse into the possibility of a different kind of democracy.

THE YEARNING FOR SOLIDARITY

Many times, I was asked what the outcomes of the discussions at the tables were. The main points of the discussions at all the tables were sent to a central editing desk, resulting in a central document highlighting the main topics raised by everyone. However, this document, which can be found in various versions online, was not the most important outcome. What remained from this entire event was the deep yearning of citizens for solidarity. The discussions around the tables enabled meetings that would not have happened otherwise. Professional facilitation ensured that people listened to each other without trying to confront or flatten the discussion whenever they heard something different from their worldview. This created a sense that it was possible to be together even when there were disagreements. The facilitators encouraged everyone to express their unique perspectives and helped each table find what united them, not just what divided them. Even today, 13 years after the event, I occasionally receive emails or phone calls from people who participated, telling me how it changed their worldview and enabled them to initiate community initiatives and create impact by inviting all stakeholders together and to overcome barriers. Round tables have become a simple, accessible and accepted tool for public participation processes, community building, vision formation, etc. Democracy has evolved, but much work is still needed to make sure that people's voices are heard and taken seriously by those who have the power to rule. Belonging to a community starts with a feeling of self-worth and a sense of contribution. We need leaders to understand this and facilitate the transition.

INITIAL REFLECTIONS ABOUT THE NEEDED LEADERSHIP

Back to the event, when everyone was seated around the tables and the square was filled, it was time to kick off the event. Unlike protests where the spotlight is on speakers competing to inspire the crowd with meaningful and hopeful words or sharp criticism, the action at the roundtables event was centered around the tables, in the listening and quiet, noninflammatory conversation.

Therefore, when my friends and I took the stage to greet everyone and start the event, most people didn't know who we were and didn't expect us to say anything important. We kept our greetings brief and left the stage as quickly as possible – though the experience of standing on stage and feeling the power of a square full of thousands of people listening to you was electrifying and mesmerizing. After stepping down from the stage, I went aside to take a moment alone to process the magnitude of the event. It was the first time I had ever felt such emotions, and I was at a loss for words.

A few days after the event, my thoughts became clearer, and the words came to me. I realized that it was a moment of leadership. Until that day, I hadn't acknowledged myself as a leader. I was just a consultant to leaders. In that moment, I was, truly, a leader, and it was an amazing thought and feeling – not because of the scale and power of the event, though that also played a role, but mainly because of the type of leadership I demonstrated alongside my partners. It wasn't charismatic leadership expressed in a fiery speech. It wasn't directive leadership telling people what to do. It was connective leadership, inviting people to get to know each other beyond cultural differences, political views and ethnic backgrounds. It was leadership that provided people with a space and a simple method to have this dialogue. It was leadership focused on the possibility that what connects us is greater than what separates us. And perhaps this is the kind of leadership the world needs in this era.

Having explored the concept of participatory democracy and its potential to bring people together around shared goals, we must ask ourselves, what is the kind of leadership that can make such inclusive and diverse collaborations thrive? In the next chapter, we delve into 'Connective Leadership,' a leadership style that not only acknowledges our differences but also uses them as a strength to create unity and achieve collective goals.

We will explore examples of leaders from both the past and the current times who have embodied this approach.

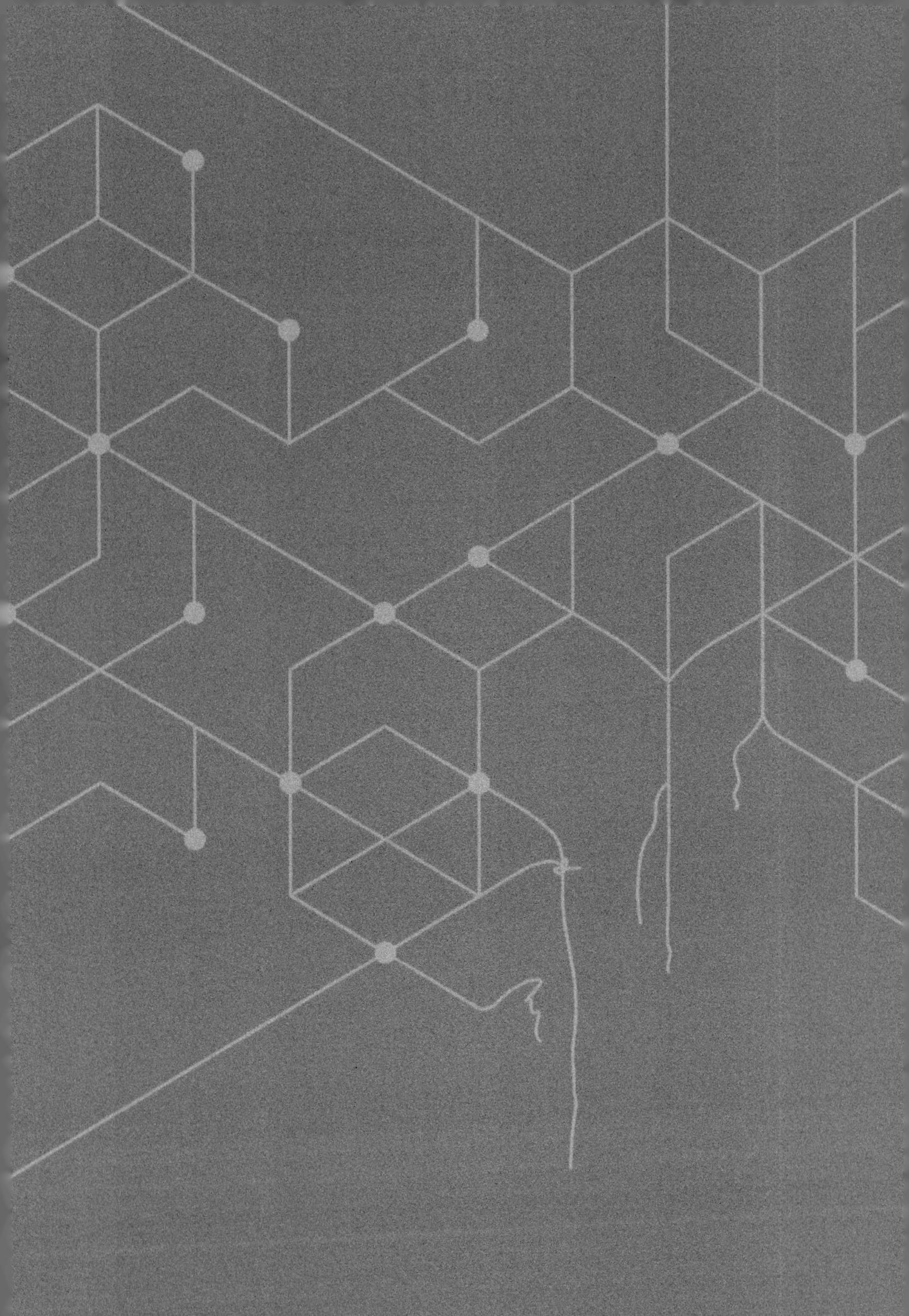

CHAPTER 15

CONNECTIVE LEADERSHIP

A STORY OF CONNECTIVE LEADERSHIP

The excellent Netflix series about Barack Obama showcases many scenes highlighting Obama's choice to walk the connective path rather than the divisive one. He chose to represent all races and not just focus on African-American voters. This approach disappointed some traditional African-American leaders in 2008 but won him the hearts of a large majority of American citizens from all ethnic groups.

One fascinating moment in the series describes a meeting of Republican candidate John McCain, who ran against Obama in the 2008 election, with a crowd of fans during a campaign rally. This meeting took place against the backdrop of the smear campaign claiming Obama was a Muslim collaborating with terrorists. During a Q&A session, a woman got the microphone to ask a question: "I don't trust Obama ... I read about him, and he is not ... he is ... Arab ..." McCain's response was remarkable and not at all self-evident in today's political climate. McCain did not allow the woman to finish her question. He took the microphone from her and answered firmly: "No, ma'am, no, ma'am, he is a family man and a decent citizen with whom I have fundamental disagreements, and that's what the campaign is about ..." Obama eventually won, thanks to the hope and connective message he offered the American nation, and perhaps also thanks to McCain, who refused to degrade the campaign to low places that would have severely damaged the ability to create connection and live together. McCain saw the danger of division and the potential of connection – and that was perhaps more important to him than winning the presidency.

WHAT IS CONNECTIVE LEADERSHIP?

Leadership researcher Jean Lipman-Blumen explains in her book, *Connective Leadership*, that the world has entered the 'Connective Era' in the 21st century (Lipman-Blumen 2000). Throughout human history, we experienced the 'Physical Era,' where physical conditions such as forests, oceans, rivers and mountains either separated or connected people. This was followed by the 'Geopolitical Era,' where ideological and political boundaries defined the connections and separations between individuals. Now, in the Connective Era, the accessibility of technology and transportation has eliminated geographical distances, fostering diversity and variety among people from different cultural, geographical and ideological backgrounds. This high connectivity results in diverse environments where different types of people are compelled to live together and collaborate to achieve common goals.

The complexity of cooperation increases with diversity, which requires effective management. In the past, leaders during the Physical and Geopolitical Eras primarily guided homogenous groups within defined and confined areas. However, leaders in the Connective Era face a much more intricate challenge: uniting diverse individuals with varying perceptions and expectations, connecting them through numerous virtual and physical channels, to collaboratively achieve common goals.

CONNECTIVE LEADERSHIP IN A VUCA WORLD

Reality is even more complex than that. Today, we commonly refer to our current situation as an ongoing VUCA environment – a term coined by the American military in 1987 to describe Volatility, Uncertainty, Complexity and Ambiguity in the world. When we combine society's diversity and high connectivity with the characteristics of VUCA, it creates a world where traditional concepts like management, planning and control, which were developed in the 19th and 20th centuries during the geopolitical era and the height of the industrial revolution, seem increasingly outdated. In the midst of this doubt, we must focus on identifying the aspects that still function effectively within the VUCA framework.

Basic human needs remain unchanged. We still require security, but we can no longer find it solely in certainty. We still need love, but it cannot come just from pleasing others. We still seek to belong to something greater than ourselves, yet we can no longer expect this belonging to be stable, defined and clear, as everything is in constant flux. So, what enables us to fulfill the basic need for belonging? We need to cultivate mental flexibility and self-acceptance. Flexibility to understand that belonging is temporary, and farewells are a natural part of life. Flexibility, as John Lennon aptly put it, in recognizing that "life is what happens to you while you're busy making other plans." ("Beautiful Boy," *Double Fantasy*, 1980). Self-acceptance is to find joy in the journey, not just in reaching the destination.

PRACTICAL GUIDELINES FOR CONNECTIVE LEADERS

- **See the potential of togetherness**: Prioritize the positive potential of unity and collaboration. Recognize that the strength of the group lies in its diversity and the unique contributions of each member.
- **Identify and leverage strengths**: Continuously identify the unique strengths and 'gifts' of each individual. Encourage and facilitate opportunities for team members to express these strengths within the collective framework.
- **Create psychologically safe spaces**: Design and maintain safe environments where people from diverse backgrounds can meet, interact and build connections. Ensure that communication within the team is safe and inclusive. Everyone should feel empowered to express their needs, dreams and fears, with consideration for the feelings and perspectives of others.
- **Invest in shared spaces**: Dedicate resources and thought to the creation and ongoing development of physical shared spaces. Ensure the design is conducive to open dialogue and collaboration over time.
- **Build a shared leadership team**: Form a leadership team that doesn't rely on one person. Distribute responsibilities across the team to foster a sense of shared ownership and accountability.
- **Balance expression and belonging**: Skillfully manage the tension between personal expression and the need for a cohesive social fabric. Encourage individuality while promoting a sense of belonging and mutual respect.

EXAMPLES OF CONNECTIVE LEADERSHIP IN PRACTICE

A great example of flexibility and self-acceptance was demonstrated by the renowned gymnast Simone Biles, who chose not to compete in some events at the Tokyo 2020 Olympic Games due to mental health concerns. Biles' decision may have drawn criticism from circles that prioritize achievement above all else, but it resonated with millions of people worldwide. Her actions validated the idea that the end goal does not justify the means and that prioritizing one's mental wellbeing is more important than even an Olympic medal. This is an example of connective leadership.

Another example of connective leadership in our time is the leadership of Jacinda Ardern, Prime Minister of New Zealand, who led the world's most successful campaign against the coronavirus. One of her first actions upon her appointment was to appoint the most diverse government in New Zealand's history: out of 20 cabinet members, eight were women, five were from the Maori minority (Maori make up 14% of the population), three from the Pacific minority (7.5% of the population), and three were LGBTQIA+. The swift action to diversify and represent all the populations making up New Zealand in the government is a leadership act demonstrating a unifying and connective leadership perception.

HISTORICAL EXAMPLES OF CONNECTIVE LEADERSHIP

The pages of history are filled with stories of leaders who brought about the liberation of people, equal rights, and social and environmental justice. Mahatma Gandhi led the nonviolent resistance movement for India's independence. Emmeline Pankhurst spearheaded the fight for women's suffrage in England. Martin Luther King, Jr. championed the civil rights movement for Black Americans. Nelson Mandela fought against apartheid in South Africa and became its president. Harvey Milk advocated for gay and lesbian rights in San Francisco. Malala Yousafzai continues to fight for women's rights in Pakistan against the Taliban.

These leaders managed to resonate with people beyond those directly affected by their struggles. Martin Luther King, Jr. enlisted a significant portion of white Americans to his cause. Nelson Mandela touched the hearts of people worldwide, who connected with the anti-apartheid struggle and effectively pressured South Africa to change. Harvey Milk rallied straight people in San Francisco to support his fight for gay and lesbian rights. Research shows that the success of a social change movement requires mobilizing at least 25% of the directly affected group. From there, the support graph spirals out of control, turning into a massive wave of indirect and external supporters, leading to the movement's success and achievement of its goals.

To succeed, it is crucial to reach people who are not the direct beneficiaries. This requires the movement's leaders to connect with the hearts of people from all groups and align their struggle with universal values that resonate with everyone. It demands connective leadership that enables every individual to find their place within the larger group without losing their identity and with the ability to empathize with others outside their own group.

THE FUTURE OF CONNECTIVE LEADERSHIP

In today's world, nationalistic and isolationist movements are gaining ground, driven by a rising fear of the unfamiliar and a desire for self-preservation. From Brexit's push for separation to the popularity of far-right parties in Europe, these movements reflect a broader trend toward disconnection and division. Leaders around the world are tapping into nationalist sentiments, appealing to fears and reinforcing borders rather than fostering unity and collaboration. This global shift suggests that, in many places, the call to embrace empathy and interconnectedness has become more challenging, yet more crucial than ever.

However, these developments underscore the necessity, not the failure, of connective leadership. The challenges of our time – climate change, global pandemics, refugee crises and economic inequality – are inherently transnational and complex, requiring collaborative solutions that transcend borders and ideologies.

Consider the leadership of individuals who have chosen the connective path. Jacinda Ardern's inclusive approach to governance in New Zealand, and Barack Obama's efforts to unify diverse groups in the United States, illustrate the potential of connective leadership. Historical figures like Nelson Mandela, Mahatma Gandhi and Martin Luther King, Jr. have shown that leaders who bridge divides and inspire collective action can drive profound societal change.

These examples illustrate that connective leadership is not only possible but essential for addressing our global challenges. By fostering dialogue, understanding and collaboration, connective leaders can create resilient and innovative communities. They can guide us through uncertainty, not by exploiting fear, but by cultivating hope and shared purpose.

In conclusion, while the current political landscape may seem to favor division, the enduring need for connection and collaboration highlights the critical role of connective leadership. The future calls for leaders who can transcend boundaries, embrace diversity and inspire collective action. Embracing connective leadership principles will pave the way for a more inclusive, resilient and hopeful world.

As we reflect on the need for connective leadership in today's fragmented world, it becomes clear that our collective wellbeing depends on leaders who can bridge divides, embrace diversity and inspire collaborative action. From the examples of great leaders, both past and present, we see that it is possible to build a more inclusive and connected world. This journey is not just for formal leaders; it is for the leader within each of us, to embody the principles of empathy, connection and courage in our daily lives. By stepping into this role, we hold the potential to reshape our societies into places where everyone can truly belong while being their unique selves – where empathy becomes the cornerstone of our shared humanity.

EPILOGUE

So much has happened since I started writing this book: the COVID-19 pandemic, the Russia-Ukraine war, the Israel-Hamas conflict, two failed assassination attempts on Trump, civil war in Sudan, catastrophic floods and other climate change impacts that claimed around 12,000 lives in 2023. It feels as if the pace is accelerating, and we are constantly experiencing more and more stress. This is the world we created, and this is what we will pass on to future generations. Can we change our ways? Can we slow down and choose a different path?

The Belonging Paradox is a call to see our situation with new eyes. It is an invitation to open our hearts to each other, especially to those we fear and see as a threat. It is an urgent call for collaborative action that starts with radically changing how we understand and practice being together.

The Belonging Paradox is just a teaser, a hint, a baseline for much more research and development around how we change the foundations of our societies and humanity at large. It is a call to invent a new kind of economy that prioritizes the greater good over the narrow benefit of the few. It is a call for technology innovators to create new systems that respect our attention rather than compete for it, to develop technologies that protect the social fabric rather than tear it apart. We need societies that celebrate diversity, connectivity and belonging rather than view them as threats.

The Belonging Paradox is also an invitation for personal reflection on how we conduct our own lives. How can we rediscover our empathy in a world that suffers from an empathy deficit? How can we find ways to be fully ourselves and express our uniqueness in a manner considerate of our neighbors and other community members?

The Belonging Paradox is my way of expressing my deep worry but also my belief in the basic goodness we all share as humans. Like many others, I feel worried about the world we will pass on to our children, but I also know we have the potential to create a better world where humans live in harmony with nature and each other. A world that allows everyone to be a creative member of society. A world that allows everyone to belong while being uniquely themselves. A world where empathy is the foundational ingredient in everything we do.

BIBLIOGRAPHY

Bakan, D. 1966. *The Duality of Human Existence: Isolation and Communion in Western Man.* Beacon Press.

Brown J., Isaacs D. 2005. *The World Café: Shaping Our Futures Through Conversations That Matter.* Berrett-Koehler Publishers.

Chan, M.M.Y., Han, Y.M.Y. 2020. "Differential Mirror Neuron System (MNS) Activation During Action Observation With and Without Social-Emotional Components in Autism: A Meta-Analysis of Neuroimaging Studies." *Molecular Autism* 11 (72). doi:https://doi.org/10.1186/s13229-020-00374-x.

Cinga. 2021. *The Loneliness Epidemic Persists: A Post-Pandemic Look at the State of Loneliness among U.S. Adults*. Cinga Newsroom. Accessed October 5, 2024. https://newsroom.thecignagroup.com/loneliness-epidemic-persists-post-pandemic-look.

Csikszentmihalyi, Mihaly. 1991. *Flow: The Psychology of Optimal Experience: Steps toward Enhancing the Quality of Life*. New York: Harper Collins Publishers.

Deloitte. 2023. *Uncovering Culture - A Call to Action for Leaders.* Deloitte DEI Institute and the Meltzer Center for Diversity, Inclusion and Belonging, NYU School of Law. https://www2.deloitte.com/content/dam/Deloitte/us/Documents/about-deloitte/dei/us-uncovering-culture-a-call-to-action-for-leaders.pdf?dl=1.

Duhigg, Charles. 2016. "What Google Learned from Its Quest to Build the Perfect Team." *The New York Times Magazine*, February 25. https://www.nytimes.com/2016/02/28/magazine/what-google-learned-from-its-quest-to-build-the-perfect-team.html.

Entringer, T. M., Gebauer, J. E., & Paulhus, D. L. 2022. "Extracting Agency and Communion From the Big Five: A Four-Way Competition." *Assessment* 29 (6): 1216-1235. doi:https://doi.org/10.1177/10731911211003978.

Gladwell, Malcolm. 2002. *The Tipping Point: How Little Things Can Make a Big Difference*. Back Bay Books.

Lipman-Blumen, Jean. 2000 . *Connective Leadership: Managing in a Changing World*. Oxford University Press.

Scharmer, C. Otto. 2009. *Theory U: Leading from the Future as It Emerges*. Berrett-Koehler Publishers.

Timimi, Sami. 2009. "The Commercialization of Children's Mental Health in the Era of Globalization." *International Journal of Mental Health* (Taylor & Francis, Ltd.) 38 (3): 5-27.

Yoshino, Kenji. 2006. *Covering – The Hidden Assault On Our Civil Rights*. Random House.

DANNY GAL is a leadership coach and social entrepreneur with over 30 years of experience working with leading companies like HP, Monday.com and Teva Pharmaceuticals. He has facilitated transformative dialogues, including bridge-building efforts between Israelis and Palestinians and the 1,000 Roundtables Dialogue, Israel's largest public dialogue event.

A graduate of Harvard Kennedy School, Danny combines empathy, systems thinking and innovative leadership strategies to address the global challenges of disconnection and polarization. In *The Belonging Paradox*, he shares practical insights and inspiring stories to help leaders and individuals create a more connected and empathetic world.